The Writer's Guide to Editing Fiction

How to Polish your Writing – a comprehensive guide including a 171-tip checklist

by editor, creative writing tutor, and author

Morgen Bailey

Kind regards, Morgen

Published by Morgen Bailey

Table of Contents **Page**

The checklist of 171 tips for making your writing shine is:

1. Accents, slang etc.
2. Active verbs
3. Adjectives
4. Adverbs
5. Ages
6. Ago vs before vs earlier
7. All and both
8. Among vs amongst
9. And vs then
10. Animals
11. Any more vs anymore
12. Anyway or any way
13. Arms' length or arms' length
14. Apostrophes
15. As vs so/then or because/when
16. At all
17. Began to / started to
18. Besides vs beside
19. Body movements
20. Capitalisation
21. Chapters
22. Characters' names
23. Characters speaking
24. Characters thinking
25. Chronology
26. Clichés
27. Collapsed ~~to the ground~~
28. Colons
29. Colours (colors)
30. Commas in general sentences
31. Commas between adjectives

164. Who vs whom
165. Who's vs whose
166. Word choice
167. Word count
168. Words that mean the same
169. Wordy phrases
170. Why use four words when one will do
171. Zzz…

These include many of the 'errors' I have found in my clients' novels over the years so wanted to share them with you to help you with your writing ongoing.

Introduction

Hello. I'm Morgen Bailey, a writer, freelance editor, writing blogger, former writing group chair, and creative writing tutor for Northamptonshire County Council's Adult Learning sector covering the whole county of Northamptonshire, England, teaching 19 to 99-year-olds… and beyond!

I have been helping authors refine their novels, short stories, poetry, scripts, and non-fiction since 2008 and have worked with independent and traditionally published writers at every stage of their career.

I shall be guiding you through some of the processes needed to take your (primarily) novel or short story from first to final draft so that it's good enough to submit to a competition, agent, or publisher.

I write novels (currently three published, five in the works) and short stories (eight collections published so far) so I am also experienced to help you as a writer, not just as an editor.

In this book we will be looking at:

- the components of your story;
- points of view;
- tenses;
- the power of three: start, middle, end
- another power of three: characters, setting, plot
- conflict and pacing
- polishing your writing – 171 tips for making your writing shine;
- the layout of your book;
- and finally (a summary checklist)…

This book is suitable for…

- Writers of any age and experience;
- Writers of novels and short stories (predominantly – it will help scriptwriters and poets too);
- Writers looking to have their writing taken seriously!

So do join me on this journey to make your writing get noticed.

Before I leave you to go through this guide, I'm going to set you a challenge…

An editing book should be perfect, shouldn't it? Should you find any mistakes, do let me know (my details below) and I'll reward you with a free Kindle (or other eBook format) of any of my books (see https://morgenbailey.wordpress.com/books-mine) or, if you prefer, a free online course. You can choose from the options on https://morgenbailey.wordpress.com/courses/online-courses).

I hope this book is useful to you. I'd love to hear how you get on.

Morgen
morgen@morgenbailey.com
www.morgenbailey.wordpress.com

***

The Writer's Guide to Editing Fiction – How to Polish your Novels and Short Stories

You've just finished your first draft, or your on your umpteenth draft, having worked hard for months on your manuscript and you've had a friend or family member to go through it, give you feedback and then – when you've made the amendments you've agreed with – it is your 'baby' after all – it's ready to go. But is it?

I'm very honest with my clients about their writing (I say I'm firm but fair) so I will be honest with you. Even with this guide, I'd still recommend employing a professional editor but here I've provided you with the tools to buff your manuscript to within an inch of its life.

A lot of people think that they can write the first draft then send it to an editor for them to sort it out (or agent / publisher, or even self-publish it!). Of course you can, but you would be best to work on it before you submit it. It would cost you a lot less where the editor charges per hour rather than per word (I'm the latter – it's much fairer; you know the costs upfront and that never changes unless you have another service) but you will learn more about your story if you go through it several times. There will also be less work for you to do when it comes back from the editor and you can concentrate on what they have found in the 'perfect' version… there will always be something.

And editing isn't just about chopping… or the infamous 'killing your darlings', it is about ensuring that the story works, your characters have depth, the dialogue is realistic, the location interesting, and so on.

Writing a Story

Why am I telling you how to write a story? I'm not, as such.

You may have bought this book before you've written the story, perhaps you've started but are struggling.

You may be the type of writer who writes a few pages then goes back and edits before continuing. Personally, I don't recommend it because the writing is too 'fresh'. If you're like me and don't have a particularly retentive brain (a nice way of saying "a hopeless memory"!), you just want to get the idea down.

Every writer has their different way of writing; some (myself included) just get an idea and run with it... we're called 'pantsers'. Others plan meticulously. It is said that Frederick Forsythe plans his novels for a year and produces book-sized outlines. For me, I just want to get on with the writing, and most of the authors I've interviewed (over 800 since 2011, which you can read at https://morgenbailey.wordpress.com/guests/blog-interviews) have said they are the former. They love to write so they don't want to delay that. That said, I think the best way is somewhere in between; to make some notes, sketch a synopsis so you know where you are going. Agents want synopses anyway (most one page, some two – single-spaced is fine).

Whichever method you go for, you have to do what's best for you but I would recommend making some notes so you have a vague idea of what's going to happen.

Things change along the way but with some form of plan you have a structure upon which to hang your plot.

And don't worry too much (or ideally at all!) about your first draft. No one would put you in front of a canvas and tell you to paint a Dali or Vettriano (my favourite artists). Likewise, no one would put you in front of a piano and expect you to play like Beethoven or Satie.

NOTES:

Writer's Block

Some (including established writers) say that writer's block doesn't exist. Comparing it to plumber's block is very valid but I'm sure there isn't a writer alive (or dead!) who hasn't got stuck at some point in their novels... perhaps not so much in short stories because there's less to get stuck on. For me, when this happens, I write (type) 'more here' and continue with a later part of the book.

When my first draft is done, I can then search for all the 'more here's and fill in the details because I know what's happened from A-Z in order to get F, M, and Q.

If you struggle with any other part of the book, then move on to something completely different; another story, brainstorm new ideas (for the story you're stuck on or new ones), or do something other than writing, but don't leave it too long to come back to it. It will be easier with time passed. Then would be a good time to write the synopsis / plan if you've not done so already.

I talk more about writer's block and help you get ideas in my 1,000-prompt '365-day Writer's Block Workbook' series. See https://morgenbailey.wordpress.com/books-mine/writers-block-workbooks for more details.

NOTES:

Points of View

The point of view, or viewpoint, is from whom the story is told. In any section there should be one main character from whom we get to experience the story. There are three main points of view:

- First person, e.g. I, we;
- Third person, e.g. he, she; and the lesser-known
- Second person, e.g. you.

First person

First person point of view has the main character (the protagonist) sharing his or her story with us.

You see what happens through their eyes which can feel very inclusive and comforting (unless they're under threat!).

The limitation of using this viewpoint is that you can only have the main character's observations and their opinions on other characters.

You can't skip into another character's head unless you move to that person in the next (or later) chapter or section (blank line then non-indented first paragraph).

Use first person if you want that intimacy but if that character isn't able to share vital information, e.g. anything that happens when he / she isn't present, then either alternate the points of view (best to use first / third point of view rather than two first person points of view) or make the entire story in third person.

NOTES:

Third person

Third person is the most popular, and therefore widely used, point of view. Most stories will talk about characters as 'he' or 'she' (and their given names).

There are two types of third person point of view:

- Third person limited – from the relevant main character's point of view only so there is no reflection from inside anyone else's head.
- Third person omniscient (he / she – from anyone's point of view but ensure you leave a blank line and start a new section (non-indented first paragraph) in the other character's point of view.

NOTES:

Second person

Wikipedia explains second-person as: 'The **second-person narrative** is a narrative mode in which the protagonist or another main character is referred to by second-person personal pronouns and other kinds of addressing forms, for example the pronoun "you".'

Second-person point of view isn't widely known or used, and a lot of readers (and therefore editors) don't like it because they feel it's accusatory.

Personally, I love it and if you do, I'd recommend using it for short stories or small sections within your novel but not for the whole thing. Jay McInerney's 'Bright Lights, Big City' (see below) is the most well known of second-person viewpoint. It's only short (c. 100 pages) but quite hard going… in my opinion, and I love second person. As I said, it's not for everyone but find an editor (or competition judge) who likes it and you could be in with a chance of success because not many people write it.

Bright Lights, Big City was released as a book in 1984 then, four years later, became a film starring Michael J Fox. The novel starts…

> You are not the kind of guy who would be at a place like this at this time of the morning. But here you are, and you cannot say that the terrain is entirely unfamiliar, although the details are fuzzy.

One of my second-person stories (The Dark Side) starts…

> You struggle to breathe as you look down at the cot. You know he won't be far away. It's only a matter of time. Your heart quickens as you hear gravel shifting. A large car – his Daimler.
>
> You've got it all planned but of course there's no guarantee... What if...? It's no good thinking what if? you tell yourself.

You only have one chance. To escape. Be free. Alive again.

You stand up straight and your hands tighten around the bundle you hold close to your chest. It's the key to everything. This is what it's come to, you know he's here to kill you, take your child, his heir.

*

You can read the rest of my story at http://www.smashwords.com/books/view/101139, and I have tips on writing the second-person viewpoint at https://morgenbailey.wordpress.com/writing-101/2ppov.

There are a number of adventure books which use second person, the most famous being by Ian Livingstone and Steve Jackson. One is a series called 'Fighting Fantasy'. (https://en.wikipedia.org/wiki/Choose_Your_Own_Adventure) An optional task from one of those books is to…

- think of a number between 1 and 300 then turn to that number.
- Read the passage then follow the instructions for up to five moves, writing down the next numbers and make brief notes as you go along **in the form of a map** and no more than five words per location.
- Now write a second-person story following that route, changing specifics that could be classed as 'plagiarism', i.e. named locations or other characters.

There are also Doctor Who 'Decide Your Destiny' books so you could do the same if you have (or buy) one of those.

NOTES:

So, a checklist regarding point of view:

- Are you telling your story in the correct point of view?

- Does each section have one main viewpoint character and not get into any other characters' heads?

- Are you struggling to get everything across from this character? If so, try rewriting that part in another character's viewpoint.

- Should another character be the main point of view character for that scene?

- If you need to switch to another character's head then leave a blank line, start a new (non-indented) paragraph and do the same thing again when you switch back to the original character, or another point of view.

NOTES:

Tenses

There are three main tenses:

- Past tense (the most popular);
- Present tense (the second most popular);
- Future tense (rarely used).

Past tense (I went / you had / they were)
Past tense is the most used tense. It describes something that has already happened.

Most works of fiction are written in third person past tense and it is certainly the tense that most editors prefer.

There was a spate of present tense in recent times but editors seem to have tired of it and will invariably prefer past tense.

Present tense (I walk / you hear / he swims)
As I mentioned above, contemporary writing is being more and more written in the present tense, and while some editors aren't partial to it, it does bring some immediacy to your writing.

From a reader's point of view, it is like they are taking part in the action as it happens.

Both tenses are quite easy to write providing you don't slip from one to the other. Novels are sometimes written with different tenses in alternate chapters and that can work well.

Future tense (I will see / you'll think / she'll travel)
Like second-person viewpoint, future tense is rarely used in published works as it is quite difficult a tense to sustain for a lengthy piece. I would again however suggest that you try it because you may well enjoy the challenge.

NOTES:

Summary of Points of View and Tenses

Point of view	Tense
First person (I)	Past (I went / you had / they were)
Second person (you)	
Third person limited (he / she – from their point of view only so there is no reflection from inside anyone else's head)	Present (I walk / you hear / he swims)
Third person omniscient (he / she – from anyone's point of view but ensure a paragraph gap when changing points of view)	Future (I will see / you'll think / she'll travel)

Task: to write a sentence using the following:

- First person, present tense:

- Third person, present tense:

- First person, past tense:

- Third person, past tense:

- Second person, future tense:

Did you find the latter the most difficult?

What do you think of second person as a point of view?

NOTES:

The Components of your Story

The Power of Three: beginnings, middles, ends

Beginnings

The beginning is one of the most important aspects of your story.

If you don't grab your reader from the off, then the chances are that they won't read on. It is often tempting to introduce the main character – which you should do in chapter one (or the first couple of paragraphs) – and include a lot of backstory to show how they got to the point of the story.

Personally, I don't mind 'It was a dark and stormy night.'* It sets the atmosphere although it's not particularly action-packed but it hints at an unsettling scene.

*https://en.wikipedia.org/wiki/It_was_a_dark_and_stormy_night explains "It was a dark and stormy night" is an often-mocked and parodied phrase written by English novelist Edward Bulwer-Lytton in the opening sentence of his 1830 novel Paul Clifford. The phrase is considered to represent "the archetypal example of a florid, melodramatic style of fiction writing", also known as purple prose.
(I talk about purple prose later).

Below are some tips on writing beginnings. Do these match your story's beginning?

- Beginnings should invariably start with the action. Unless it's relevant, don't have your character getting to the scene where the action then takes place. You can always flashback to how they got there later, to the 'backstory'.
- 'Action' doesn't necessarily have to be movement but it does have to be the conflict or dilemma, e.g. they're told they're about to lose their job, they're 'dumped' by their partner via text message / email etc.
- Avoid information 'dumps' where you're giving too much to the reader too quickly, especially where it's irrelevant – do

they need to know where the main character (protagonist) went to school? Sure, if it's relevant and if they're still there, or they're reflecting back on it for a reason.

- That said, when you're writing a first draft it doesn't really matter how you start. It's often said that an author can either delete (or better still cut / paste into another document) the first two chapters because the action starts in the third.
- If the first two chapters are important, they can be slotted in later. Sure, we need to know who our protagonist is, the dilemma they're facing, an indication of setting and another character fairly soon as they're bound to have an interaction with someone else at some stage and it's often another character (the antagonist) that causes our protagonist the problem.
- It's important to introduce the main character on the first page (novels) or first couple of paragraphs (short stories), including his or her name. Don't say 'he' / 'she' unless there's a reason to reveal his / her name later.
- Think about the point of view and tense you're going to use. The most popular is third person (he / she) and past tense (he / she went).
- The shorter the opening sentence, the better. If you can make it one word that would grab the reader more, unless it was an insipid word such as 'Darn' or 'Okay'. Would you read on? Probably, but does it make an impact? Not so much. Make it pop. If a story started 'Wimp.' or 'No!' would you be more intrigued and keen to continue?

NOTES:

Traditionally published example beginnings

Below are some of my favourite opening sentences.

Think about why they work and how you could grip your reader in the same way.

- Character: 'Once upon a time, there was a woman who discovered she had turned into the wrong person.' – Anne Tyler's Back When We Were Grownups

- Character: 'There was a boy called Eustace Clarence Scrubb, and he almost deserved it.' – C. S. Lewis' The Voyage of the Dawn Treader

- Setting: 'It was a bright cold day in April, and the clocks were striking thirteen." – George Orwell's 1984

and my favourite…

- Timing: 'It was the day my grandmother exploded.' – Iain M Banks' The Crow Road

Below are a few suggested beginnings I have created for you. You could use them as they are or change to any extent (especially the names); and of course they don't have to be the beginning of a story, they could appear in the middle or even be the final sentence. ☺

1. Joe's fingers stuck as they / he ran through…

2. The wilted flowers reminded Abbie of…

3. Clara's hand stung from the slap…

4. Long, short, it didn't matter…

5. "Yeah, we're finally here!"…

6. As she fled the scene…

7. I was sure it would all end in tears…

8. Josie felt the dark cloud loom over her…

9. It should have been me…

10. Susan's gloves were threadbare.

Middles

The middle of a short story isn't usually too difficult because you have one plot, a small cast of characters, and your job as a writer is to provide the tools for solving the conflict that appeared at the start, but writing the middles of novels is hard.

You have to join the beginnings with the ends in such a way that your reader cares about your characters and wants to know what happens next, so they turn the page, and keep turning.

In a novel you have several threads running through the story so you have to keep track of where you are at and that the reader is following you.

It's tempting to let things plod on with the character continuing their journey to resolution but 'plod' is the operative word.

So, how can you fix your 'saggy' middle? Think about what's happened so far…

- What is the conflict or dilemma facing your character?
- Is it a complex enough one that when the character tries to do something about it they make matters worse?
- Does something outside of the character's control make it worse?
- Have they achieved their initial goal but find that it's not enough and now they want something else?
- Do you have enough characters?
- Can you introduce a new character that will complicate (in a bad or good way) the plot?
- Do you have too many characters – could you kill off one of them?
- You could be really brave and kill off your main character partway through the novel and make a secondary character come to the foreground. That way, the reader knows that no one is safe.
- Have a twist. Something / someone isn't what they seem.
- Perhaps one of your minor characters (not your main character) could divulge some information unknown to the main character up to then (it could be known to the reader providing you've told it from the minor character's point of

view) that changes the stakes.

Maybe your middle has already happened.

What I mean by this is that your epic novel could actually be less epic than you planned and you should now start thinking about wrapping up the story, ensuring that your character resolves their problem (it can't be solved by someone else solely, they can help) and tying up all the threads. We'll be talking about endings later in this guide.

http://www.keepwriting.com/tsc/magnificent7plotpoints.htm which summarises a story's seven plot points as…

- Number One. The Back Story haunts the central character.
- Number Two. The Catalyst gets the character moving. It's part of the story's setup.
- Number Three. The Big Event changes the character's life.
- **Number Four. The Midpoint is the point of no return or a moment of deep motivation.**
- Number Five. The Crisis is the low point, or an event that forces the key decision that leads to your story's end.
- Number Six. The Climax or Showdown is the final face-off between your central character and the opposition.
- Number Seven. The Realization occurs when your character and/or the audience sees that the character has changed or has realized something.

NOTES:

Example mid-point turnings

- Star Wars: At the midpoint, a tractor beam pulls Luke (and his friends) into the Death Star. This is obviously the point of no return. There's no going back to the farm now. (from http://www.keepwriting.com/tsc/magnificent7plotpoints.htm)

Two from https://www.storymastery.com/articles/30-screenplay-structure:

- Erin Brockovich: Erin and Ed* file the lawsuit, risking dismissal by the judge, which would destroy any hope of a settlement.
- Gladiator: Maximus arrives in Rome, determined to win the crowd as a Gladiator so he can destroy Commodus.

*see later names references to not using the same first letter.

http://thestorydepartment.blogspot.co.uk/2007/03/that-mid-point-thing.html has four examples:

- The Untouchables: The mid-point sequence happens halfway the movie (ironically, not all midpoints really do), it changes the course of the story (Ness is no longer after Capone but after his accountant) and it takes place in a very different environment / change of scenery from the rest of the movie. And indeed: catching the accountant does get Capone in court.
- Jaws: The midpoint reversal forces him to change tactics (different direction): he must go and attack the shark in its own habitat. It brings a fresh turn to the movie with a change of scenery and the stakes are heightened because we are now fighting the killer on his own territory. What's more: the protagonist is under greater jeopardy because he can't swim...
- North By Northwest: The single most memorable scene of this film sits right in the very middle: the famous crop-duster scene. Again, an entirely new setting in the movie, with hardly any other characters around. While most of the movie is rather talky, this sequence offers pure visual cinema with

minimal sound design, then gradually picking up the pace and finally (literally) exploding in a symphony of action and music. The reversal: Roger Thornhill learns that Eve has betrayed him.

- The Queen: A moment of realisation (with a lot of symbolism) leads to the decision to chase the deer away in an attempt to save its life from the hunters. The parallel with Princess Diana's end becomes even more apparent when it turns out the deer was shot by a group of hunters after a chase on a neighbouring land (France?). The Queen has witnessed something that has changed her view and we see it externalised in her lukewarm response to the Queen Mother's statements about the British people in a following scene.

Karel at http://thestorydepartment.blogspot.co.uk/2007/03/that-mid-point-thing.html then goes on to name some 'failings' in stories:

Script Editors' Top Ten:

1. long descriptions; 2. lack of practical insight; 3. too many characters; 4. too many subplots; 5. over-writing; 6. passive protagonist; 7. weak antagonist; 8. not enough obstacles; 9. absence of logic; 10. breach of genre rules.

Karel's Top Ten:

1. weak protagonist; 2. lack of conflict; 3. lack of subtext; 4. lack of turning points; 5. shifting point of view; 6. on-the-nose dialogue; 7. too clever dialogue; 8. camera direction; 9. lengthy scenes; 10. bad use of parentheses.

Other helpful websites talking about story middles:

- http://www.sfwa.org/members/bell/writingtips/winter0708.html
- http://www.novel-writing-help.com/plotting-the-novel.html
- http://storyfix.com/story-structure-steries-6-wrapping-your-head-around-the-mid-point-milestone
- https://www.storymastery.com/articles/30-screenplay-structure
- http://thescriptlab.com/features/screenwriting-101/1712-story-plot-points-twists-and-turns
- http://www.crackingyarns.com.au/2010/07/30/midpoint-stakes-supreme-ordeal-identity-essence

---

NOTES:

Ends

Things to remember about your story's ending:

- Endings are just as important, if not more so than beginnings. They have to tie up all the loose ends – main plot and sub-plots – unless you're writing a series where questions will be answered in later books, you need to make sure that any queries the reader may have had about the plot through the book are answered by the end.
- You can leave an ending open where it is left to the reader to imagine what happens next but only up to a point (and mainly only in flash fiction / short stories). If your character hasn't solved the dilemma then it's not an ending. They could have solved the problem only to find that there's another one; this could then be continued / concluded in the next book (the sequel).
- They also need to leave the reader with some emotion; relief, pleasure, at the very least satisfaction. How many times have you thrown down a book (a paper one rather than electronic, hopefully) because you'd been disappointed by the ending. Not only have you invested money in what you've just read but also several hours of your time.
- Of course if the beginning and middle weren't good enough to keep you motivated you may not have reached the end, but if they were then it's even more important to reward the reader for making it thus far. It wasn't all a dream (thank you, Bobby Ewing) or the antagonist a figment of the protagonist's imagination (aka Stephen King's Secret Window). Everything has to make sense, to the point where the reader says, "Oh yes, of course!" or they go back looking for the clues and find them. This is vital for genres such as crime where a reader hasn't (hopefully) guessed who the identity of the killer, thief etc. The last thing you want your reader to feel is cheated so don't have the killer only introduced at the end. They have to have been in the novel for some or all of the time, even in plain sight or as a minor figure.
- In a novel, you can have an epilogue (where you say what happened next, e.g. some time later) but, like a prologue

(pre-chapter one), some readers don't read them. That's not the writer's fault but you risk the reader missing out on some information.

See below for example endings and some tasks you might like to try…

Example endings

- Conclusion: 'The scar had not pained Harry for nineteen years. All was well.' J.K. Rowling's Harry Potter and the Deathly Hallows
- Open-ended: 'The man in black fled across the desert, and the gunslinger followed.' Stephen King's The Dark Tower

Endings – twists (beware – there are plot spoilers!)

- The Empire Strikes Back (1980): Luke Skywalker comes face-to-face with Darth Vader at Cloud City, engaging the Dark Lord in a fearsome light saber battle that costs him his hand.
  The Twist: Darth Vader, embodiment of all that is evil, reveals himself to be Luke's father.

- The Usual Suspects (1995): When a botched heist leaves a boat full of corpses at the door of inspector Dave Kujan, he ropes in limping conman Verbal Kint for a protracted haul across the coals. As he leans on the hapless Kint, he learns the legend of a monstrous crime lord known as Keyser Soze.
  The Twist: Convinced he has wrung the cripple dry, Kujan sends Kint on his merry way before realising he's just been fed a pack of lies. Meanwhile, out on the street, Keyser Soze shakes off his limp and rides off into the sunset.

- The Sixth Sense (1999) Young Haley Joel Osment suffers from an unusual condition – he sees dead people. Fortunately, Bruce Willis' friendly psychologist is on hand to help him through it. Not that things are all roses for Bruce, whose relationship with his wife has got so bad that she barely seems to acknowledge his presence.
  The Twist: Bruce was dead all along, which is why only Haley Joel could see him.

Endings exercises

NB. you can change the points of view and / or tenses.

Write a short piece with one of the following endings. Ensure that the information you've given the reader up to that point leads them to the conclusion, explains the clues, etc.:

- And that was why I'd gone alone. (first person, past tense)

- She / he laughs as she / he finally realises the joke. (third person, present tense)

- She / he left the room, not realising what was underneath the bed. (third person, past tense)

- I'd known all along it hadn't been the postman. (first person, past tense)

- She / he opened the drawer and screamed. (third person, past tense)

NOTES:

Another Power of Three

Other than a start, middle, and end, there are three main elements to a story: your characters, settings (locations), and plot.

Here, we'll look at those and other aspects.

Characters

Regarding the characters in your story:

- What is his / her motivation?
- What is their backstory?
- What would the reader like / dislike about your character?
- Have you got more from the characters' viewpoint, i.e. they are physically doing or saying something (a 'show') rather than from the narrator ('tell').
- Do you have enough / too many characters? Do they help or hinder the main character? How does that affect the story?
- Are your characters the right ages? By that I mean, do they act their age… if they're supposed to. You could have fun with that.
- Do you have them looking in the mirror to describe themselves? If so, don't. It's a cliché (and seen as lazy).
- Is your dialogue realistic? Remove all the description (including 'he said' / 'she said'). Does it still make sense?

- Are your characters individual? Friends speak very differently to each other than strangers will. The latter will more formal, have more complete sentences. In real life, we pause (I er…), interrupt each other (That's not f–!)
- Speaking of individual characters, your reader should care enough about the main character that they want them to be okay by the end of the story. There will (and should) be characters that they don't like (the baddie – the antagonist at the very least) but it shouldn't be the main character they dislike or your reader won't get to the end to find out that they are okay.
- How has what has happened to your character during the story changed them? Have they learned a new skill or become a better person?

To help you create a character, find a picture of someone either from a magazine or online (Google, for example, has an images section) then complete the form below:

Name / nickname		
Nationality		
Age / job		
Hair colour / style		
Height / build		
Favourite music		
Favourite food		
Regular saying		
Relationship		
Children		
Siblings		
Best friend		
Aspirations		
Quirks		
Hero or baddie?		

NB. Hero = protagonist, baddie = antagonist.

Characters' names

Which names have you used for your characters? Do you favour particular letters for the beginning of the characters' names?

Readers usually remember names by the first letter so having too many that look similar (e.g. Tim, Tom, Jim etc.) or start with the same letter and are similar lengths, e.g. Diane, Dean, Derek.

I provide my clients with a table in which to insert their characters names as they create them (or I do so as I go through their manuscript).

I've pasted an example of the table overleaf but will explain…

- Create a six-column matrix, the first column being your A to Z, the second and third are dedicated to females (the first being the character's first name, the second the surname) then two for male characters and the final other names such as town, objects, titles etc. After each name put the chapter number you first insert / encounter the relevant name.
- Once you have completed the table, you will see which letters you use regularly and which ones you've not used so you can rename the minor characters to even things out.

Letter	Female – first name (& chapter number)	Female – surname (& chapter number)	Male – first name (& chapter number)	Male – surname (& chapter number)	Others (locations etc)
A					
B					
C					
D					
E					
F					
G					
H					
I					
J					
K					

and so on…

Your main character (the goodie) will be your protagonist. The baddie will be the antagonist. The way to remember is that pro means positive and anti means negative.

I talk more about characters later in the ‘polishing your writing’ checklist.

NOTES:

Settings

Regarding your settings (locations) in this story:

- If your story is set in a real location, is everything accurate? Someone reading your story will know the place and be only too keen to tell you (or worse, leave a review) when you've got something wrong.
- Provide enough information but not too much. Unless you've created a new world, most people will know what an office looks like, what a field looks like so you don't need to go into too much detail.
- Don't forget the five senses; what can your characters hear where they are… smell, see, taste, touch. Does the location have any connection with the five senses? I regularly drive past a sewerage works to the side of a dual carriageway. I ensure my windows are closed and heating / cooling system is off. How could you incorporate something like this into your story? Although it's not a big deal in itself, it is a form of conflict.
- Outside and inside locations can also affect the story and the five senses. The weather can cause a conflict. Imagine someone trying to move house in a force ten gale.
- How does the location itself affect the story? Is it restrictive? Is it a huge area that the characters find intimidating? Ian Rankin, for example, uses Edinburgh as another character. Where have you chosen for your story? Would moving the location elsewhere make it a different story? I'm not suggesting you do that if you have finished the first (or later drafts) but something to consider when creating new pieces.

Settings exercises

Pick a short story, any short story…

1. Having read the short story, complete the following:

- Name the settings mentioned;
- Were there indoor and outdoor settings?
- If at all, how did the locations affect the story?
- Why did the author pick those locations?
- Would you have changed any of them?

2. Pick one of the following films / TV series and describe the (main) location / setting and how the setting is key to the plot (or if it isn't why it doesn't make a difference). Does having the story set in a real place make it easier to describe?

- At sea: Titanic, Pirates of the Caribbean, Peter Pan (the scenes with Hook);
- Dry land (fictional places): Shrek, The Simpsons, Batman, The Wizard of Oz, Buffy;
- Real places: Sleepless in Seattle, Sex in the City, Iron Man, Peter Pan, Doctor Who;
- Another planet: Jupiter Ascending, Babylon Five, Dune, Superman, Thor, Passengers, The Martian.

NOTES:

Plots

I could fill a whole book on plots but below are some points to check with your story:

- Is it a feasible plot? Fiction is something that could happen but hasn't necessarily. It has to be believable, even if you've set it on another planet.
- Does it have a start, middle, and end? This may sound a crazy thing to ask but sometimes you may have a start and middle but a lacking ending. This is fine for flash fiction, although it still shouldn't be lacking(!) but your reader should be satisfied. They've invested many hours reading your story and don't want to feel cheated.
- Are all the threads (story plots) resolved by the end? If you're writing a series, the main thread has to conclude but others can be left open.
- Make a list of your main plot points, e.g. 'Fred has a problem, he tries to work out how to fix it but it creates another problem; he doesn't have enough money. His friend Tom offers to help but Fred has his pride and wants to solve the issue on his own. He realises he can't so enlists the help of Tom's wife Lisa to talk to Tom without letting on that Fred has conceded to his offer.' Does it all work?
- Then going into more detail, write a sentence for each chapter. Is every chapter relevant to your story?
- Once you have finished the drafts and you're happy with the story, go through it again. Is every paragraph vital to the plot? Every sentence? Delete anything that isn't relevant.

NOTES:

Conflict and Pacing

Conflict

Every story has to have conflict. It is said to put a man (or woman!) up a tree and throw rocks at him (her).

In the British magazine 'People's Friend' we may find that Freda's washing machine has gone wrong. That is conflict.

It's not as high drama as your characters being held up in a bank or kidnapped but it's still a problem. We will look at character motivation in more detail later, but Freda immediately has the motivation she needs to get the washing machine fixed.

Have her call in a plumber who fixes it and you have no story. Have her watch what he does so that she can fix it herself if it goes wrong, then we sort of have a story. Have her go to evening classes to learn home and car maintenance, then you have a story.

Characters should have learned by the end of the piece. Readers should be educated, entertained, and feel some emotion… the three 'e's.

I talked about characters earlier and invited you to kill off one of your main characters. In the movie 'GI Joe', Channing Tatum's character was killed off in the first ten minutes. Us, the viewers, then know that no one is safe. It heightens the tension.

We now look at conflict in order to increase the pacing – and your reader's page turning – of your stories…

NOTES:

Pacing

Pacing is made up of peaks (the action) and troughs (the slow points).

What makes your reader turn the page?

While a thriller will have a stronger sense of pace than a saga, you don't want the whole book to just be all peaks. It would be too tiring. I read James Patterson's 'Step on a Crack' (one of his collaborations with Michael Letwidge) in one sitting and was exhausted!

I'm predominantly a crime writer (I also write chick lit novels and short stories in most genres) so I tend to use crime examples. In a crime novel there will often be a dead body in the opening (or at least the second) chapter then the police will investigate. There might be chases (peaks) hunting the killer, interrogations (troughs, unless there's a fast exchange of dialogue), and James Patterson is a great example here as he often alternates chapters between the police (the protagonists) and the killer (the antagonist).

NOTES:

Pacing Exercise 1 – which works better?

- Joe and Cheryl were on their way to an appointment. They said nothing as they waited at traffic lights.

Would you read on? Where's the conflict? Whose story is it?

From Joe's point of view (because he's mentioned first)...

- Joe had lost count how many times he'd urged Cheryl to hurry up. Would it kill her to be ready for once? She knew how important this was yet her priority had been deciding what to wear. He gripped the steering wheel tighter as the light turned red.

Better? If so, why? So far, the pacing is quite slow but we can feel the tension.

And in Cheryl's point of view?

- Cheryl wanted to scream at Joe. He never seemed to understand why the little things mattered so much. It was all about feeling right but Joe's recent actions made Cheryl wonder whether **he** had any feelings left.

Note: this time we have a more active verb: 'scream'. This adds to the action and therefore the tension.

So, whose point of view does it work best in?

Sometimes if a scene isn't 'working', it's because you're telling it from the wrong character's point of view.

How about their conversation just in dialogue (no description)?

"Cheryl! We're going to be late."
"It's okay. There's plenty of time."
"Just pick something, will you?"
"I want to look nice."
"Why? What does it matter?"

We understand the tension between the couple but does it feel as if it's getting anywhere?

In most cases, it works best if we are inside the heads of the characters (one at a time: if we're in Joe's head, we can't be in Cheryl's).

- Cheryl slammed the wardrobe shut as Joe slammed the front door.

Now we have tension. What happens next?

NOTES:

Pacing Exercise 2 – which works better?

- Tom and Susan finished their cups of tea then left the room. They went to their car and got in. The road was clear so they drove off.

Would you read on? Where's the conflict? Whose story is it?

From Tom's point of view…

- Tom said nothing as Susan put down her cup. He knew if he said anything more she'd cause a scene. He picked up the car keys and shut the front door behind him. Putting on his seatbelt, he stifled a yawn.

Better? If so, why? So far, the pacing is quite slow but we can feel the tension.

And in Susan's point of view?

- It's a lie, Susan wanted to say as the cup wobbled back on to the saucer. She wanted to tell him he was wrong, that everything he'd said hadn't happened. He snatched the car keys and slammed the front door before she had time to follow.

Note: this time we have a more active verb: 'slammed' instead of 'shut'. This adds to the action and therefore the tension.

So, whose point of view does it work best in? Sometimes if a scene isn't 'working', it's because you're telling it from the wrong character's point of view.

How about their conversation just in dialogue (no description)?

"It's not true."
"That's what she told me."
"She's lying."
"Why would she lie?"
"She's never liked me."

We understand the tension between the couple but does it feel as if it's getting anywhere?

In most cases, it works best if we are inside the heads of the characters (one at a time: if we're in Susan's head, we can't be in Tom's).

- "It's not true." Susan watched the cup wobble back on to the saucer.

Now continue the story…

NOTES:

Pacing Exercise 3 – Examples from Television and Film

The following are examples of film or TV scenarios. Write a paragraph for one from each batch (i.e. one fast-paced and one slow-paced), best describing the action taking place – in either first-person viewpoint (as if you're that character) or third-person narration.

Fast-paced

- Bruce Banner has just turned into the Incredible Hulk and is on the rampage (Hulk – TV & films)
- Jack Traven (Keanu Reeves) and Annie Porter (Sandra Bullock) are in charge of a runaway bus, with a bomb on board and can't go ~~above~~ below 50mph (80km/h)! (Speed – film)
- Jack Bauer is chasing a terrorist and has 24 hours to save the world (24 – TV series)
- Norman Bates (Anthony Perkins) stabs Marion Crane (Janet Leigh) through her hotel room's shower curtain (Psycho – film)

Slow-paced

- Bruce Banner tries to pacify himself to avoid turning into the Incredible Hulk (Hulk – TV & films)
- John Rambo (Sylvester Stallone) is stitching up his arm (Rambo: First Blood – film)
- SFPD Inspector Harry Callahan (Clint Eastwood) is standing over a bank robber (Albert Popwell) and is about to say, "Do I feel lucky? Well, do ya, punk?" (Dirty Harry – film).
- Wonder Woman (Lynda Carter) has lassoed a baddie and is talking to them. (Wonder Woman – TV)

These are still scenes of conflict just not as action packed as the earlier examples.

Regardless of what is happening around them, think about what your character is afraid of…

- snakes?
- silence?
- a gun being pointed at them?

How does this impact the pace? How does it differ if your character is the one chasing or being chased?

NOTES:

We shall shortly be getting to the checklist of ways to polish your writing but first we are going to do some chopping. Yay!

Editing Exercise 1

Below is a piece of 200-word flash fiction I wrote especially to be edited. Your task (should you accept it) is to read the story, then edit to 100 words (or as near as you can get it):

Sarah put the book down. She was fed up with reading about yet another perfect woman who said she didn't want the perfect man who had been talking to her all night. The story was boring.

Sarah went to make a cup of tea. She put the kettle on. She put a teabag in a mug and stood looking through the kitchen window outside into her back garden. There were no birds but that was because there was a cat in the back garden.

The kettle boiled and Sarah made herself a mug of tea. She added two sugars and stirred the mug.

Her husband Frank wasn't due home until seven… in a couple of hours – it was now five o'clock. He caught the train from London so wouldn't even be on the train yet.

With the mug of tea in her hand, she returned to the lounge and decided to read a little bit more of the book. She decided that she would give it ten more pages then stop reading.

She had just returned back into the lounge, put the mug down and picked up the book, and was going to read some more when the phone rang.

Now edit it down to 100 words:

And now down to 50 words. You may have to rewrite it.

While the end story may not be a masterpiece, it has hopefully shown how much you can chop out and yet it still makes sense.

Don't be afraid to be brutal… or to rewrite something completely.

I'd recommend not having your characters bored because it encourages the reader to be too, especially where your characters are doing mundane tasks such as making a cup of tea.

There are too many sentences starting with 'she' or 'Sarah'… how would you fix that?

And the split infinitives, e.g. She put down…

Watch out for repetition. How many more 'more's do we need?

And where are the colours?

NOTES:

Editing Exercise 2

Below is another 200-word flash fiction, this time in second-person point of view. Unlike the first story, I didn't write this one to be edited. It features in my first volume of 'Fifty 5pm Fictions' (see https://morgenbailey.wordpress.com/books-mine/short-stories/fifty-5pm-fictions-collections for more details).

Again the task is to read the story, then edit to 100 words (or as near as you can get it) and finally 50 words. The checklist appears after this exercise so you might like to leave it for now, go through the checklist, then edit this with skills you've learned. Alternatively, edit this now then go through the checklist and see whether you would have done anything differently thereafter. You may well find that with such a small piece that there isn't much (if any) difference but an option for sure.

You saw her mouth form a smile, right before your right foot pressed down on your blue Ford Mondeo car's accelerator. That movement of yours soon changed her expression, didn't it? Didn't think you had it in you, did she?

You had tried before, different method; wrapped her favourite red and black scarf around your wrists like you'd seen in the movies, except that it was too big, it was too awkward, and she had grunted and turned over, burying her neck in the pillow, leaving no clear skin open.

You had stood there for ages, staring at her, looming over her skeletal frame, wasting away from the disease eating her inside out.

You had finally had enough when she'd started refusing to eat, neither of you having the strength to argue.

You loved her with all your heart, so you'd taken her to Devon, as you had every summer, to that little out-the-way place with the crumbling cliffs.

Any doubt you had disappears as your Ford Mondeo car gathers pace. She takes your left hand and squeezes it, and you look at her face. It is no longer pale, no longer sallow, and her eyes have never been bluer.

Now edit it down to 100 words:

And finally down to 50 words. You may have to rewrite it.

Did you find that more difficult because it wasn't written for this exercise, or easier because you'd already edited the first version?

NOTES:

And now for the

editing tips checklist…

Polishing your writing – a 171-tip checklist for making your writing shine

Absolute / Absolutely – see 'Excess words'

1. Accents, slang etc.

Keep your accents (especially slang) to a minimum. If a reader can't understand what your character it saying, they'll lose interest and potentially stop reading the story.

Your reader will want an easy and entertaining read. Make it too much like hard work and they won't be encouraged to read anything else you've written.

There are words that are often used more in certain countries, for example, I've noticed that 'Look' is popular at the start of Australians' dialogue sentences.

2. Active verbs

I talk about verbs and adverbs throughout this book and so forgive me if this is repeating myself but by using active verbs, it changes your writing from two-dimensional to a three-dimensional so it's important to reiterate. What do I mean by an active verb? If you have a character walking slowly, the reader might struggle to picture them but have them plod or shuffle then it's more specific. Replace pushed with thrust, lunged or sprang (depending upon the context) then it implies a quicker action. Have the character 'edge' then it shows caution.

3. Adjectives

Adjectives are, in order: Number, quality, size, age, colour / color, origin, and type.

So, if you say you have ten large books, you do not need a comma since ten is a number and large is a size. The adjectives are of the same weight or degree. If, on the other hand, you say you have a shiny, sparkling ring, you will need to put commas between them since shiny and sparkly both describe the quality of the ring.' Also see 'Commas'.

When comparing using adjectives, the general rule is that if the adjective is short (e.g. black) it should have -er on the end, e.g. it was blacker than he'd expected. If the adjective is long (e.g. attractive), you'd say 'she was more attractive than he'd expected'. Generally, it's how it sounds. 'she was attractiver' wouldn't sound right, would it. (please say "no")

4. Adverbs

Stephen King's writing guide / autobiography 'On writing' has been the most suggested book in the interviews I've conducted (mentioned earlier).

Amongst other things he's notoriously against adverbs ('ly') and I agree. In 'completely dead' you wouldn't need the 'completely' because dead says it all (see later for 'Excess Words'), and a character doesn't need to be 'sighing wearily' because the sighing tells us enough, but adverbs are necessary where the context isn't clear.

If you're using including adverbs after dialogue, e.g. "That's great!" she cried happily, you can not only lose the 'happily' but – providing we know it's her speaking' – you can lose the 'she cried', especially because I'd not recommend using crying unless there are tears involved. See below for more tips on dialogue but if you can read out your dialogue without the he said / she said, then they can go.

Again it's all about clarification and fine-tuning. Once you've written your first draft, I'd recommend searching for the 'ly' words, and seeing how many you can delete. I bet you at least half of them can go. Some great articles on adverbs include:

- https://suite.io/kenneth-burchfiel/1a2b2p0
- http://chiseledinrock.blogspot.co.uk/2011/05/stupid-writing-rules-watch-adverbs.html
- http://www.quickanddirtytips.com/education/grammar/how-to-eliminate-adverbs
- http://www.writingforward.com/writing-tips/writing-tips-abolish-adverbs and
- http://www.humankinetics.com/flguideonweb/NitToPick32UnnecessaryAdjAdv.htm.

5. Ages

Ages are fairly straightforward. If you have someone who is mid twenties, he / she would be twenty-five years old. Better still, end the sentence at the age. We don't need the 'years old'.

If you are referring to someone in the third person, you would say a twenty-five-year-old.

6. Ago vs before vs earlier

If you're writing fiction in the present tense you can say something was ten years ago but if you're writing in past tense you'd use 'before' or 'earlier'.

The easy way to remember the difference is that with past tense, it already happened **earlier** than / **before** today.

7. All and both

It's easy to include the words 'all' and 'both' when you don't need them.

Say your character is unlocking a car, you don't need to say 'all the doors', just say 'the doors'.

Unless he / she is only unlocking one or, say, half of them, it's assumed all are unlocked. If you can remove 'all' and the rest makes sense, then it can go.

The same goes with 'both'; if you have two of something, by saying 'they' or 'them', you don't need to include the word 'both'.

NOTES:

8. Among vs amongst

Like 'while' or 'whilst', you can use 'among' or 'amongst' in your writing.

A reviewer of my chick lit novel, The Serial Dater's Shopping List, said I had too many 'whilst's in the book. I have since re-edited it and replaced them with 'while's.

I didn't have any 'amongst's but I would have changed them too.

https://en.oxforddictionaries.com/usage/among-or-amongst explains that among appeared in the English language before amongst but I'd recommend using the former as 'amongst' and 'whilst' feel old fashioned… as they're two letters shorter so printers will be pleased because they take less space.

9. And vs then

'and' is an accompanying word whereas 'then' implies time passing.

You don't need to use both in your writing so it's worth searching for that phrase.

If you're using Word, it's Alt F (or Edit / Find) on a PC, or Command F on a Mac then type "and then" in speech marks so it only picks up that phrase rather than each word separately.

10. Animals

They say never to work with children or animals but at one time or another we include them in our stories.

It's obviously easy to tell whether a child is feminine or masculine but harder to tell the gender if an animal (this is where fantasy writers say, "if they have one"!) so rather than describe the animal / creature as him or her, stick with it, unless the gender is clear / important.

'It' is especially useful when you already have a him / her so helps avoid the reader getting confused as to whom the him / her refers.

11. Any more vs anymore

If you were to say, "Do you have any more cakes?" then that would be two words. If there aren't any, the reply would be "I don't have any more", but it could also be "I don't have any cakes anymore" so 'anymore' in that instance means time. So remember time is one word (syllable) and quantity is two (syllables).

12. Anyway or any way

http://www.dailywritingtips.com/anyway-any-way-or-anyways explains that 'anyway' is an adverb and provides the example of 'Marshall's grades have slipped, but he plans to apply to Harvard anyway.' Any way, however, is a is a paired adjective and noun meaning any particular course, direction, or manner: 'Chloe is willing to help Marshall prepare for the SAT in any way she can.'

13. Arms' length or arms' length

As http://www.oxforddictionaries.com/definition/english/arm's-length says, it should be singular, i.e. arm's length.

14. Apostrophes

I could fill this whole book with when and where to use apostrophes but the http://www.apostrophe.org.uk/page2.html page explains that: yes for possessions e.g. Tom's hat and abbreviations like it's for it is – no for plurals e.g. Tom's hats). When it comes to oddities like 1980s, again it's referring to several years (1980, 1981 etc) so it's plural and no apostrophe.

NOTES:

15. As vs so/then or because/when

I've added this because one of the client novels I was editing had a phrase, 'he found it as he turned back' which could be read as him having found it before he turned back (the 'so' or 'then' version of 'as') or that he'd found it when he turned back (the 'because' or 'when' version of 'as'). Isn't the English language great. :)

16. At all

'at all' at the end of negative phrases often detracted from the impact of the 'not' or 'nothing' so I remove them. 'at all' works best as emphasis, e.g. 'This is not good, Sam, not good at all.'

Authorial voice – see 'Voice'.

17. Began to / started to

Only have characters begin / start to do something if they're going to be interrupted. If they do something, have them do it, so just use the active verb e.g. he sang instead of he began to sing / started to sing. Apart from cutting down the word count, it brings the reader (and the character) quicker to the action. This is something I often spot in the novels I review. Search your longest piece of fiction – how many 'begin', 'began', 'starts' or 'started' do you have that you could chop?

18. Besides vs beside

http://www.grammar-monster.com/easily_confused/beside_besides.htm has a great explanation on the difference, but beside is a synonym (similar word) for next to or near, and besides is a synonym for furthermore or in addition to.

19. Body movements

Before you snigger, no, I'm not being smutty! There are phrases connected with the body that can be trimmed, e.g. he shrugged his shoulders, nodded his head, pouted her lips, she replied with a big grin on her face. In those instances, the 'his shoulders', 'his head', 'her lips', and 'on her face' can go because the phrases still make sense – we know shrugging can only be done by shoulders, nodding by a character's head, pouting by the mouth, and grinning by the face.

Also, our hearts are only in one place so you don't need to have a character having 'his heart thumped in his chest'. You can stop the sentence at 'thumped'.

'corner of his / her eye' is a cliché so have a character see or spot something. Less is more.

20. Capitalisation

http://en.wikipedia.org/wiki/Capitalization#Titles says, "In English, some authors/publishers capitalize the first word and the last word of titles. In addition, they believe that all nouns, pronouns, adjectives, verbs, adverbs, and subordinate conjunctions should be capitalized.

Articles and coordinating conjunctions are not capitalized, while sources disagree on the capitalisation of prepositions. For example, no prepositions are capitalized in the title of a book, a movie, or a play according to some style guides, for example the Chicago Manual of Style. The APA style guide, for example, however says: Capitalize major words in titles of books and articles within the body of the paper. Conjunctions, articles, and short prepositions are not considered major words; however, capitalize all words of four letters or more."

NOTES:

21. Chapters

How long are your chapters? Divide the story's total word count by the number of chapters. Look at those over 5,000 words.

Most readers like to complete a chapter before putting the book down, especially at night, so they appreciate relatively short chapters.

These will vary depending upon the type of story you write; a thriller will likely have shorter chapters (and shorter sentences) whereas a saga (e.g. a Catherine Cookson novel) may well have longer sentences and chapters.

Thrillers often switch from character point of view (e.g. between the police and the criminal) and location from chapter to chapter whereas sagas will have slower pacing with more description.

As mentioned earlier (regarding plots), is every chapter relevant to your story? Is every paragraph? Every sentence?

22. Characters' names

How many of your characters' names start with the same letter? Readers generally remember the characters by the first letter so I devised a character table for my editing clients for them to avoid having names that look alike on the page. It's best to use the table as you create your novel but you can always compile the table when you go through your novel for a second, third, fourth edit.

Ensure whenever you use him / her, that it refers to the last-mentioned name. You want to avoid the reader being confused.

Surnames are often used in novels but not so much in short stories, unless a character is being formal and called Ursula Harper 'Mrs Harper'. Again, try to avoid having names with the same starting letter.

23. Characters speaking

When your characters are talking to one another, you usually need a comma before their name e.g. "I didn't know that John" means that you didn't know a person called John.

If you're talking to John and you're telling him there was

something you didn't know then you need a comma, e.g. "I didn't know that, John.

Make your characters different from one another. Ethel Skinner in EastEnders got her words wrong just enough to mean something else.
https://www.youtube.com/watch?v=Bv8mg5mNH_s (go to 2m 28s) shows her saying that Charlie has been found 'decreased' rather than deceased on the M25.

24. Characters thinking

If you have a character thinking, you'd usually use italics. You can also use it for quoting names in your story, such as a restaurant or book title. Some writers write the character's thoughts in speech marks (" ") or inverted commas (' ') but your reader won't know that the character is thinking until they read the 'he / she thought' and it might confuse them. Likewise if having the speech without any indication that it is thought.

25. Chronology

Check that your story works chronologically. By this I mean that you don't have something happen on a Tuesday before something else happens on the Monday (the previous day). In my first novel, Hitman Sam, I had just that so I dated all the chapter so I knew that everything happened in the correct order.

NOTES:

26. Clichés

I always recommend avoiding clichés, especially in narration. You can get away with it with dialogue and you can certainly have one character talk in clichés so it become a trait.

In the television programme 'EastEnders', there was a character called Ethel (who doted on her dog, Willy) who often got words confused, e.g. decreased instead of deceased – see from 2m30s to 2m44s on https://www.youtube.com/watch?v=Bv8mg5mNH_s.

Cliché's include: rock solid, as white as snow, a breath of fresh air, turned on his / her heel, strong as an ox, in his / her tracks, etc.

27. Collapsed ~~to the ground~~

If you say something or someone collapses (or crumples, not crumbles) then you don't need the 'to the ground' unless they don't get that far, e.g. 'He collapsed on to the desk'.

Likewise, if someone's sitting then you don't have to say they 'sat down' because we only sit down. Just say 'sat'.

Collective nouns – see Nouns – collective

28. Colons

There's often confusion between a colon and semi-colon.

Generally if you're going to list something use a colon, if you're going to enhance or explain something you use a semi-colon, and in both cases, you use a small letter (unless a name follows) for the first word after the colon or semi-colon, e.g. He told her what he needed: a rope, goggles and a notebook.

http://grammar.ccc.commnet.edu/grammar/marks/colon.htm explains in detail and http://www.colonsemicolon.com is a great resource.

29. Colours (colors)

Instead of using standard colours, use shades, e.g. russet or scarlet instead of red. It brings the colours alive. Wikipedia (e.g. https://en.wikipedia.org/wiki/Shades_of_red) has great examples.

One of the exercises I run with my students is to get a colour chart (any DIY shop will have a supply) and pick some of the names e.g. https://www.dulux.co.uk/en/colour-palettes?gclid=CLf0keyD19ICFaQW0wodqP8Fbg has the likes of ‘Holiday Blues’, ‘Royal Regatta’ and ‘Mineral Mist’.) What could you make from that?

30. Commas in general sentences

I think we generally all know when to use full stops and commas. If you pause for breath you’ll probably need a comma. If you come to the end of a sentence, use a full stop.

A sentence is usually defined as a collection of words that make sense together. Commas are usually used before a 'but' where the rest of the sentence would make sense on its own.

If you read your work out loud, it'll be more obvious where they're needed. There's some more help on http://grammar.yourdictionary.com/punctuation/comma-usage.html, including, 'If you use a number of adjectives to describe something, you sometimes have to put commas between them.

NOTES:

31. Commas between adjectives

Whether or not a comma is required depends on the weight of the adjective. Adjectives are, in order: Number, quality, size, age, colour / color, origin, and type.

So, if you say you have ten large books, you do not need a comma since ten is a number and large is a size. The adjectives are of the same weight or degree.

If, on the other hand, you say you have a shiny, sparkling ring, you will need to put commas between them since shiny and sparkly both describe the quality of the ring.'

Where you have several items, you only need 'and' before the final item, e.g. 'There were cars, boats, and ships'.

http://opinionator.blogs.nytimes.com/2012/04/09/fanfare-for-the-comma-man

http://opinionator.blogs.nytimes.com/2012/05/21/the-most-comma-mistakes is also useful.

See http://www.quickanddirtytips.com/education/grammar/commas-with-adjectives for using commas when listing adjectives. If you can put 'and' between the adjectives then you use a comma, e.g. the big, heavy box would make sense if you said 'the big and heavy box'.

By putting a comma you're distinguishing that it was the box that was big, not the heavy that was big. http://www.grammar-monster.com/lessons/commas_in_lists.htm is also a great resource.

32. Commas in dialogue

As I've mentioned above with regard to character, when you're greeting or sometimes talking about a character, you often need a comma before their name e.g. "I didn't know that John" means that you didn't know a person called John. If you're talking to John and you're telling him there was something you didn't know then you need a comma, e.g. "I didn't know that, John."

33. Commas after 'transitional' phrases

Transitional phrases are those sentences started by words such as 'however', 'therefore', 'consequently', 'of course', etc. where they follow / explain a previous sentence http://www.grammar-monster.com/lessons/commas_after_a_transitional_phrase.htm gives some examples.

34. Commas – timing

As I've said, commas are used when a reader would pause, even for a fraction of a second. When have something after a certain amount of time, even just that fraction, you'd then add a comma, e.g. A few minutes later, Oliver burst into the room.

35. Commas with conjunctions

http://www.grammar-monster.com/lessons/conjunctions.htm explains when to put a comma before the likes of 'and' or 'but'.

Completely – see 'Adverbs'

36. Conjunctions

Speaking of 'and' or 'but', it's fine to use conjunctions at the beginning of sentences but the sentence must make sense, or be split from the previous / subsequent sentence for a reason, i.e. to make it stand out.

NOTES:

37. Context

The context is what matters. If there's a word the reader doesn't know, as long as the context of the piece means that they can guess without coming out of the story, then they will read on. They should be educated so don't be afraid to use (slightly) complicated words.

38. Continual verbs

An example of a continual verb is 'he was walking' instead of 'he walked'. Using the continual past tense can be tiring to read so unless you have the action interrupted, e.g. Simon was walking through the park when the ball hit him, then use the simple past tense. The same goes for present tense, e.g. Simon is walking through the park when the ball hits him.

39. Contractions (e.g. he or she had vs he'd/she'd)

It's perfectly fine to use contractions in writing, especially in dialogue, as long as it sounds right. You're reading your work out loud when you edit anyway (aren't you?) so you'll hear when it sounds right or wrong. For example, you'd say 'he'd known her for a year' rather than 'he had known...' (although both are correct), but you wouldn't change 'when he had to, he did it' to 'when he'd to, he did it' because you want the emphasis to be on the 'had'.

40. Copyright

As soon as you write something, the copyright belongs to you and no one else can legally plagiarise it (although if someone wants to, they will).

Your book should have a copyright statement that states you as the author, that the copyright remains with you, and should not be shared without your permission. You can find examples from traditionally published books.

The advise used to be to print off your manuscript and post it to yourself sealed then not break the seal so you can prove that you wrote it and when you posted it because of the stamp mark. These days, emailing a copy to yourself works just as well.

41. Crumbles or crumples

This is easy: biscuits crumble, people / buildings crumple.

42. Cut and dry or Cut and dried?

While 'cut and dry' is acceptable, and used, 'cut and dried' is the more standard form. It means that something is clear, easy to solve, e.g. the case was cut and dried. It's a bit of a cliché so don't overuse it.

43. Dash vs hyphen (also see 'Hyphen' below)

Hyphens (-) are generally only used to connect two words. Longer dashes (–) are used in various ways, but mainly to separate two sections within a sentence where the text between the dashes is highlighted, more so than separating it with commas, e.g. The book – the one he'd bought the day before – was amazing.

In dialogue where the first character is cut off by the second character, the long dash is used immediately after the final letter and before the close speech marks, e.g. "That's not f–"

http://keligwyn.wordpress.com/2011/11/28/puncutating-interrupted-dialogue explains further and

http://eliteediting.blogspot.co.uk/2011/08/hyphens-en-dashes-and-em-dashes.html

is another great guide on dashes vs hyphens.

http://www.chicagomanualofstyle.org/16/images/ch07_tab01.pdf is also a very comprehensive guide on hyphens from the masters of grammar.

NOTES:

44. Description vs dialogue

In most stories, there will be around 50% description and 50% dialogue. This will vary depending on the genre you are writing in, e.g. there will be more dialogue in a thriller, more description in a saga or science fiction fantasy story.

Description slows the pace whereas dialogue speeds it as well as brings the characters to life.

If I turn the page and there's a whole block of description, I tend to skim read until I get to some more dialogue. I have a poet friend, Pat (who's mentioned in the acknowledgements at the end of this guide), who adores description so settles back in her chair to savour the richness (hopefully!) of what she is about to read.

45. Dialogue: punctuation

Punctuation in dialogue is very different to normal text. There's a great set of dialogue punctuation rules at http://teacherweb.com/CT/scottsridgems/Jennes/punctuating.pdf.

The Dummies series is famous for their low-tech guides and their English Grammar For Dummies, 2nd Edition includes this topic.

46. Dialogue: tags

It's recommended that you can only go up to six pieces of dialogue (between no more than two people) without attributing it to someone. And there's nothing wrong with 'said'. Don't be tempted to look at your thesaurus and say 'Andy postulated'.

You could also avoid tags by another character saying "Oh Andy, that's…" or in the description; 'Andy laughed. "That's…".

Another practice for **dialogue** (especially if you need to distinguish between your characters) is to write a section, or even a whole piece of flash fiction, of just dialogue; no 'he said' / 'she said' but purely what they are saying. If you can write it, leave it for at least two weeks and then read the whole piece and know who's saying what then that may help the rest of your writing. Also see 'Said she vs she said' below.

And remember that when someone is speaking they should

have their own paragraph, i.e. move down to a new line for the next character.

47. Dialogue – er, um, and well

We say all these in real life but we shouldn't put them in our writing. I come across a lot of 'well's as dialogue pauses. As is the general rule, if you remove it and the remaining text is improved, then it can go.

48. Direct vs indirect action

Try and make your writing as direct as you can. What do I mean by that? Have the character (Ted) throw the ball rather than say "The ball was thrown by Ted". Also instead of saying "Ted saw the train speeding towards the car", having the train speeding towards the car means you're closer to the action.

49. Door vs doorway

When you have a character entering a room, they go through the doorway rather than through a door, unless they're a ghost. If saying 'doorway' doesn't sound right, find another way of phrasing what you want to say.

50. Each other's or each others'

http://virtuallinguist.typepad.com/the_virtual_linguist/2010/03/each-others-or-each-others.html explains that 'each other' behaves like a single pronoun (think of it as 'each one' so the correct use would be each other's.

NOTES:

51. Easily-confused words

http://www.grammar-monster.com/easily_confused_words.htm has a long list of easily-confused words (e.g. affect / effect) and explains the differences. Speaking of which...

52. Educate your reader

Have you educated your reader? Most children's books will be educational but subtly so that the children aren't aware that they are learning. The same can be said for books for adults.

I'm sure you've read novels (and perhaps short stories) where you have learned something. Take crime, as it's my main genre… unless you are an expert at something, the writer will hopefully inform you. Like children's books, this should be subtle. No one, unless reading a 'how to' book. No one wants to be told facts, we want to be shown. I talk about research later, but it's tempting as a writer to include a lot of the research you've found. If it's not relevant, don't include it.

Don't be afraid of using words that your readers might not know. While you don't want them to go to their dictionary every few minutes, as long as they can follow the context of the story, they shouldn't be pulled out of the story. What you want to avoid is for them to leave and move on to another writer because you've confused them.

53. Effect vs affect

http://www.elearnenglishlanguage.com/blog/english-mistakes/affect-vs-effect says, "Affect is a verb with several different meanings" (which the page lists) and "Effect is most commonly used a noun".

54. Ellipses

These are the ... dots which always come in threes. If you use a computer package such as Word, you'll probably find it automatically changes the three individual dots to a set of three dots (so your cursor would only move one space instead of three when you go over them).

If you're using them in dialogue where the character trails off (if they're interrupted, you'd use a long dash), then the three dots come immediately after the final word but if you are using them in text where you are leaving out a word or section, then the ellipses appear on their own (see http://grammar.ccc.commnet.edu/grammar/marks/ellipsis.htm for a fuller explanation).

55. Endings

I talked about endings earlier in this book but they're potentially the most important part of your story.

In flash fiction or a longer short story, you may not have one but just leave the piece open-ended so the reader can imagine what happens next.

In a novel, however, they have to leave the reader satisfied. If you're writing a series, you won't tie up all the threads but the major plot should be concluded or a new problem facing the characters arise.

You don't want for your reader to have invested several hours in your story only to slam the book shut (I know it's a split infinitive but 'to slam shut the book' sounds weird!) or throw it across the room because it didn't end how they wanted it to or they weren't happy with how it did end.

Some writers (PD James, Ann Cleeves to name two) have said that they write their novels not knowing the ending so that if it's a surprise to them, it will hopefully be so (and a pleasant one) to the readers.

When they (the writers) get to the end, they then go back and add in the clues and red herrings so it all works.

NOTES:

56. Every word has to count

Does it move the story along or tell us about your characters? If not, the chances are it can be chopped.

57. Excess words

There are loads of other words that you'll probably find you don't need in your writing. A few of mine are: usually, normally, especially, that, every, just, complete / completely, total / totally, entire / entirely, absolute / absolutely, really, very, right, simply, perfectly, immediately, quite, utterly, etc.

With any word, if you can remove it and the sentence still make sense, it can be chopped.

Others include 'stood' instead of 'stood up' (which other direction would you stand?), 'shrugged' instead of 'shrugged his / her shoulders' (it's the only part of our anatomy we shrug), 'thought' instead of 'thought to herself' because we don't think to anyone else, 'now' instead of 'right now', 'all' instead of 'all of', 'and' or 'then' instead of 'and then', 'much of' instead of 'pretty much of'.

How many 'perhaps' or 'maybe's do you have? In one of my novels, I had thirty-four 'maybe's but just two 'perhaps'.

The likes of 'in his life' can be chopped where you have 'never in his life' because 'never' means never, and 'up' from 'lift up' because lift is upwards.

I mentioned 'right' in the list because this is often a word that can be taken out if not needed for emphasis, e.g. 'He shouted right back.' vs 'She said it was right there.'

If you chop out any other words or phrases, do let me know and I'll add them to this list in the next edition.

58. Exclamation marks and capital letters

Try to avoid capital letters wherever you can because the reader will think that you're shouting at them. Obviously if your characters shouts 'stop' then you'd likely use an exclamation mark (and you wouldn't need to say 'he shouted' because we know he did from what he said). Don't be afraid to use exclamation marks but only one at a time, never two or three.

59. Exclamation marks or question marks

A great guide to when to use which mark http://grammar.ccc.commnet.edu/grammar/marks/exclamation.htm. If your character is asking a question, then you'd use a question mark (and you don't need 'he asked' because it's obvious it's a question). There is a fine line between a statement and a question as something like 'It is, isn't it' is more of a statement so you'd use a full stop (period) instead of a question mark and certainly not an exclamation mark and it's not pronounced enough.

60. Faint vs feint

http://oxforddictionaries.com/definition/english/feint explains **Faint** means 'only just able to be seen, heard, or smelled' (the faint murmur of voices) or 'lose consciousness', while **feint** means 'a mock attack' or 'make a deceptive movement' (I feinted to the right, then moved to the left). There was I thinking that lined pads had feint lines but looks like I was wrong (it does happen).

61. Farther vs Further

http://www.quickanddirtytips.com/education/grammar/further-versus-farther?page=all has a great explanation for the difference (think of far as a distance and further as in furthermore / additionally).

NOTES:

62. Feet vs Foot

http://www.quickanddirtytips.com/education/grammar/units-measure?page=all explains the differences (and other units of measurement).

Filler words – see Excess words

63. Five senses

By default we have sight (the action; what happens) and sound (dialogue, the noises around the characters) but see if you can include smell (good and bad), taste (again, good and bad) and touch (ditto!). How would a character react to another person's touch? Would they flinch or relax? A reader likes to imagine they are the characters and they can imagine the grass being mown, the donut being eaten.

64. Fonts

Fellow Crime & Publishment attendee Fiona Quinn has the brilliant suggestion of changing the font (or font size) so that all the text is in a different place and therefore refresh your brain so it is not too used to certain words being in a certain place. To show you how this would be effective…

Fellow Crime & Publishment attendee Fiona Quinn has the brilliant suggestion of changing the font (or font size) so that all the text is in a different place and therefore refresh your brain so it is not too used to certain words being in a certain place. To show you how this would be effective…

65. Full stop (period) spacing

Some writers put two spaces after a full stop (period), some put one. I do the latter, and it tends to be favoured that way by the industry because it – literally – takes less space, which means less pages and therefore lower printing costs. You may not think that it takes up space but sentences are an average of ten words long. http://www.dailywritingtips.com/calculate-your-average-sentence-length is an interesting article on this topic.

66. Genders

Be careful when you have two characters of the same genre that every he / she refers to the right person. An example would be, 'The train had already left before Tony saw Simon. He balked at his image.' Whose image do the 'he's refer to? Technically it's the last-mentioned male that the 'he' refers to (Simon) but Tony is the main character so more likely that it is Tony but anything that makes the reader pause (or wonder) is best avoided.

67. Genres

I started off writing short stories so wrote a variety of genres and enjoyed (and still do) doing so. Some authors stick to one genre and are happy doing so but you can run the risk of getting bored and it showing in your writing (even having a character who is bored encourages the reader to be too!).

Some authors are so famous for one genre that they publish under a different name so their readers don't expect that one genre, e.g. Iain Banks (literary) = Iain M Banks (sci-fi), Joanna Trollope = Caroline Harvey, Ruth Rendell = Barbara Vine, J D Robb (thrillers) = Nora Roberts (romantic suspense), Sophie Kinsella = Madeleine Wickham etc.

You should know what genre your story is before you submit / self-publish it. It could cross genres, e.g. James Bond stories are primarily thrillers but also crime (and a little romance!).

NOTES:

68. Glance quickly / briefly

Don't be tempted to say 'he glanced quickly' as to glance is a quick / brief movement so just say 'he glanced'.

69. Grammar

As you will have already found with this book, editing is not just about chopping but refining your writing. A lot of that has to do with grammar but don't panic if it is a weak area for you. Hopefully this guide will help you but the most important thing is that you tell a good story. The following website: https://en.oxforddictionaries.com/grammar/word-classes-or-parts-of-speech is a great grammar resource.

70. Hand in hand

To hyphenate or not to hyphenate?

Like 'time to time', 'side to side', or 'up to date', when used on their own, hand in hand would not be hyphenated, e.g. they saw each other from time to time and walked hand in hand.

Preceding a noun they would be hyphenated, e.g. a side-to-side parking slot or a hand-in-hand couple. The website http://www.oxforddictionaries.com/words/hyphen helps further.

71. Hankies vs tissues

No I'm not being frivolous… okay, just a little, but here I'm talking about language. Handkerchiefs are cloth (usually cotton) and tissues are paper. It makes a difference in a reader's mind which one you use. Likewise, words vary from language to language (Vauxhall used to produce a car called a 'Nova' which they scrapped because it means 'it doesn't go' in Spanish!).

Apart from the usual English / Americanisms such as bonnet vs hood, pavement vs sidewalk, us Brits call a bag that goes round our waist a 'bum bag' but Americans call it a fanny pack. A 'fanny' is something completely different here!

If you're creating your book or online content in English, most of your audience will likely be from the U.S. (India is also a leading market for reading) so bear in mind that whatever you write needs to make sense.

I'm English so I write in British English but ensure that the content should be clear so that it doesn't matter that the word is different. If something is in context, the reader shouldn't stumble, and they should learn something from what they read so language differences fall under that category.

72. Headed to

Something often done is to have a character 'heading to' somewhere. The occasional use is fine but if you can replace with a simpler 'walked to' or 'went to' then all the better.

73. Hear vs here

Like their, there, and they're, an easy mistake to make – because they sound the same – is here and hear. Here is a place (not anywhere else) and hear is to hear a sound.

74. He he she she

If you are talking about one character in a sentence then you can reduce the number of 'he's and 'she's, e.g. 'Frank wasn't sure but he went there anyway as he'd told Sheila he would.' You can lose the first 'he' because we known the verb is referring to Frank. Could you lose the second? Third? How would you re-write it?

75. Historical writing

When writing anything set in the past, it is vital that you get your facts right. Choose the period carefully and ensure you do all the research thoroughly. I talk more about research later.

NOTES:

76. To home or to hone

As http://www.writersdigest.com/online-editor/hone-vs-home explains, the verb "hone" means "to sharpen or make more acute," as in honing a talent. Alfred honed his negotiation skills to buy a new car at a very reasonable price. I hone my abs by doing 100 sit-ups a day. Generally, people drop it into sentences where they should use "home."

In verb form, "home" (as in "to home in on") means "to move or be aimed toward a destination or target with great accuracy." Missiles home in on targets. The leftfielder homed in on the fly ball. "Forget about the abs!" I said as I homed in on a mouth-watering candy bar.

77. Humour

You won't always have comedy in your stories but even the darkest of genres work well with some form of humour. Police often say that they crack jokes to keep themselves sane given how tough their jobs can be. How could you get humour into your story? Could you make one of your characters a joker? How would they affect the other characters? How would it change your story?

78. Hyphen (also see 'Dash vs hyphen' above)

http://www.csun.edu/~hcjou002/JHyphen.Guide.pdf has a great list of words that should and shouldn't be hyphenated. There's also a great page on hyphenating numbers on http://www.grammar-monster.com/lessons/numbers_as_compound_adjectives.htm.

http://www.quickanddirtytips.com/education/grammar/how-to-use-a-hyphen is a great resource (note: this link runs to four page, clickable links towards the bottom of the page).

Other resources include http://stylemanual.ngs.org/home/H/hyphen and for overuse of hyphens is http://www.proofreadnow.com/mar-16-2011-grammartip. An example of when to use hyphens and when not to is, 'a far-right party is typical of the far right'.

79. Impact

I talk about sentence lengths later but to make an impact, you could separate your words, e.g. instead of 'Not at all.' have 'Not. At. All.' Okay, so it's not strictly proper grammar but the character (or narrator) is making a point.

80. In a flash

'in a flash' (something happened quickly) is a cliché. If, for example, something vanishes, it's likely it happens at speed, so you don't need the accompanying 'in a flash'.

81. In front

'In front' means 'ahead' and can often be replaced by that word. 'In front' would usually be followed by 'of' and a place'. If it doesn't, e.g. 'She followed the car in front', you can say, 'She followed the car ahead.'

82. In his / her tracks

'in his tracks' / ''in her tracks' when being stopped are a cliché. Just have the character being stopped.

NOTES:

83. Inverted commas vs Speech marks

Speech marks (" ") used to be used for speech and inverted commas (' ') for everything else, e.g. titles, names, model numbers etc. but it tends to be the other way round these days, in publishing because it saves space (and therefore money) on the page. Whichever you use for speech, ensure you stick to that and use the other for all non-speech references.

I often find that close speech marks / inverted commas are forgotten so to check for this (a laborious task, I admit) then search for each letter followed by the " or ', e.g. a" or a'. As I said, it's laborious – because it picks up every possessive word (e.g. Linda's) but worth it.

84. ised vs ized

Generally, words ending 'ised' are British English and 'ized' are American English. There are of course exceptions, e.g. book-sized as we had under 'Writing a Story '.

Other differences include 'colour' vs 'color' respectively, and more major differences including 'bonnet' and 'hood'. The thing to remember is that if you use one form of spelling, you must stick to it. Even if you are a British writer, your publisher may prefer you use Americanisms because the U.S. is likely to be your biggest audience.

85. Italics

Generally, you would only use italics when a character is thinking (so it's clear to the reader that it's not dialogue or description) but you may also use it when including a title, e.g. She sailed on the *Titanic*.

86. Its vs it's

The easy way to remember the difference between its and it's is that it's is a shortening of 'it is'. 'its' is usually used for belongings, i.e. 'The car was on its last legs', although you wouldn't say that because 'last legs' is a cliché!

87. Just

'Just' is another word I come across being overused. Where you have a phrase such as 'just a hint' then 'a hint' is sufficient. Search for 'just's and you may be surprised how many you have.

88. Killing your darlings

You may have heard of this term and it literally means deleting something you are precious about. As I've said elsewhere in this guide, if something doesn't fit or you have a scene where nothing really happens, then it can go.

That said, don't delete it. Cut it out and put it in another document that you can come back to later.

If you haven't done so already, I suggest creating a document where you put all your ideas so that when you come to write something new, you're not staring at a blank screen, hopefully not anyway.

The thing to remember with any kind of writing is that everything has to progress the plot or reveal character. One of the best ways to reveal character is to have them speak or do something, especially if it surprises the reader or another character.

Make your writing as three-dimensional as you can.

NOTES:

Warwick University hosts a podcast called 'Writing Challenges' and one of the episodes is 'Murdering your Darlings'. The highlights are:

- All writing is rewriting. With fiction, the best test is to read it aloud and read it to somebody. It will test whether speech and dialogue is alive and if it animates your story.
- If some of the writing seems flat, shift sentences and paragraphs around to see which sounds more true to character. What intensifies description?
- If this doesn't help, change tense or point of view, ensure that the narrative moves forward and chop clichés or freshen the language.
- Let the story rest: leave it for a number of weeks so it feels like someone else's work.
- Quoted Annie Dullard's 'The Writing Life' (http://www.amazon.co.uk/The-Writing-Life-Annie-Dillard/dp/0060919884), Ursula LeGuin and Anton Chekov and that you should chop the first two paragraphs, sentences, chapters (depending upon length of work).
- Ending your story: write several versions of the final page; closure or open 'Chekovian image' and use the one that best suits the rhythm of your novel.
- **Challenge**: next time you read a novel, look for 'fissures' (gaps) then write a 1500-word max story that fills that gap that stays with the original subject and using the author's narrative style and point of view. Give it an open ending.

You can listen to this episode at: https://itunes.apple.com/gb/itunes-u/writing-challenges/id407477264?mt=10.

89. Language

I mention language in other areas of this book and this is about setting the language of your manuscript to ensure consistency, especially when it comes to spell checking. Your largest audience is likely to be the U.S. so you may be tempted to change your spellings (e.g. color instead of colour) and colloquialisms (e.g. car hood instead of bonnet) but if your story is set in another country with characters from that country then I would recommend sticking with the native tongue. Of course, if you have an agent and / or publisher then you may be overruled but it's your choice initially.

90. Last and past

The word 'last' can have two meanings: the final or the previous. So if you wrote 'the last book the teacher showed us' could mean that the teacher had no more books to share with the group or that the narrator is referring to the book previous to the one the teacher is currently displaying. Ensure your context is clear.

Equally, last and past in respect of time are similar. While you wouldn't say 'the past book the teacher showed us', the last week / the past week both can mean the week that took place before 'now'.

91. Less is more

As the saying goes, less is more. It's true in home design and it's the same with writing. If something can come out and what remains makes sense then be brave and go for it!

NOTES:

92. Lie vs lay

To lie is 'I lay' in past tense but in present tense, people lie, chickens lay. If you are putting down an object, you lay it down. If you are having a rest, you lie on the sofa.

Again Grammar Girl has come up trumps (to use a cliché!) at http://www.quickanddirtytips.com/education/grammar/lay-versus-lie.

93. Little did he know

My favourite film is 'Stranger than Fiction' (which most people have never heard of but features Will Ferrell, Emma Thompson, Dustin Hoffman, Queen Latifah, and Maggie Gyllenhaal) has a discussion between Will and Dustin about 'Little Did He Know'. It is best explained where there is something the reader learns but the character him/herself doesn't know yet. It can only be a second or two difference but reader love to be kept in the loop… as the cliché goes!

Look – see Accents, slang etc.

94. Lose or loose

To lose something is to mislay it. When something is loose, it doesn't fit properly. A louse, on the other hand, is something (someone) you **do** want mislay! ☺

95. May be vs maybe

The best way to explain the difference between these two is to give you examples, 'There may be more balloons this year because they have more money." "Maybe." The 'may' in 'may be' can be replaced with 'could' and the 'maybe' with 'perhaps'.

96. May or might

May is present tense which is fine in dialogue or present tense pieces but should be 'may have' or 'might have' in past tense narration. That said, it depends upon the context. If it doesn't sound right, then the chances are you need to stick with the present tense.

97. Middle age vs middle-aged

http://forum.wordreference.com/showthread.php?t=227520 explains that in general, middle-aged should be used to refer to people, and also when it's used in apposition (as a subjective complement). But middle-age can be used adjectivally with concepts. "A middle-aged man has problems." "That's a problem men have in their middle-age years." or "I'm not deaf, I'm ignoring you-- my problems are still what you'd call middle-age."

98. Mr and Mrs or Mr. and Mrs.

This is personal choice but I prefer not to have the full stop (period) after Mr or Mrs as it can look like the sentence ends there.

99. Mum or mum, Dad or dad.

mum is only Mum when being used as a name, e.g. “Yes, Mum.” It doesn’t have a capital when saying ‘her mum’. It’s the same for Dad, Grandpa etc. Ditto ‘the doctor’ vs ‘Doctor Who’.

NOTES:

100. Negatives

Do you have any negatives in your story? We write about what's there but what about something that's missing, e.g. an empty supermarket car park in the middle of the day. Lee Childs' Jack Reacher is a great example of a character with nothing to lose so create an unusual situation it will make the reader think outside their comfort zone.

101. Night time, nighttime or night-time

The correct spelling of this pairing is hotly disputed but according to https://en.oxforddictionaries.com/definition/night-time it is hyphenated and I agree.

Usually when pairing two words (that work as standalones) you would use a hyphen but it depends upon the context. If used before a noun, the words would be hyphenated, e.g. a well-known celebrity but not if saying 'the celebrity was well known'.

102. Normally, most of the time, usually

These all mean the same thing so you only need to use one in the same phrase, and sometimes it's not needed at all. Like every word when it comes to editing, if it can come out and the remaining text still makes perfect sense, then ditch it.

103. Nouns – collective

Items such as money, company, family, group, government, are singular rather than plural nouns and are therefore followed by 'is', e.g. The group is growing… The company was dissolved… The government stands firm.

The easy way to remember what collective nouns are… if you can put 'the' in front of the word then it is an ordinary.

104. Now

Most books are written in present tense so if you're tempted to write 'it was now hidden' then you're slipping into present tense. The likelihood is that you don't need the 'now', or if you want emphasis, find another word.

105. Numbers (also see 'Ages')

There's a difference of opinion as to using numbers in a word or number form; some say 1-9 should be in full (i.e. one, two... nine) but others say up to / including 99 should be in number form. I think it looks better (unless a date, item model number etc.) as a word, regardless of the number because it blends in with the text and doesn't make the reader notice it and therefore come out of the story.

For hyphening numbers, see http://www.grammar-monster.com/lessons/numbers_as_compound_adjectives.htm but a quick guide is: twenty, twenty-four, one hundred, a one-hundred-year-old.

House numbers, e.g. He walked to Number 14 isn't a title or name so should be 'number fourteen' and you can usually lose the 'number' where it's been established that the fourteen refers to the house.

106. of the

There is often no need for 'of the' when referring to a noun, e.g. 'the handle of the saucepan' where you could instead say 'the saucepan's handle'.

NOTES:

107. OK okay?

I'd recommend changing OK to Okay (at the start of a sentence), or okay if not the starting word, so it doesn't feel so much like shouting. I know OK is only two letters but it's best to avoid capitals where possible.

The best way to search for your oks are by putting a space or " or ' before ok otherwise you'll reveal all the looks, books etc. You could put a space either side, which will likely find some, but most will be at the start of dialogue (so " or ' before it) or have a comma or full stop (period) after it.

108. Once and once more

Once has more than one meaning; 'on one occasion' and 'sometime ago'. Where you put it within the sentence can change the meaning of that sentence, e.g. 'I told him once that he...' could mean that I'd told him on one occasion or I told him some time ago but by moving it to before the verb, e.g. 'I once told him that he...' (or once upon a time...), it makes it clearer that it was a historical event.

'Once more' is the same as 'again' so why not use 'again'? If you feel 'once more' is better for the context you have, then go for it.

109. On his / her heel

'on his heel' / 'on her heel', when it comes to a character turning, is a cliché. Just have them turning, and just round rather than around, and the latter usually implies a full circle.

110. Page breaks

I often receive manuscripts where the chapters have been separated by blank lines rather than page breaks. That's fine if you're submitting to a publisher or agent but when it comes to publishing, a paperback book is a different size to a (Word) document so your chapters won't always (often) start where you want them to because the page size will have been changed.

When uploading a Word document as an eBook, it will look right but when someone comes to read it on an eReader, the screen is that much smaller so they will find that at least one page between chapters is blank.

If you are using Word, click on 'Insert' on the top menu toolbar then take the first option, Break, then Page Break. If you have previously inserted blank lines you can then delete them.

111. Paragraphs

Paragraphs will vary in length. The shorter the paragraph the better as it leaves more white space on the page. Approximately ten percent of the population – and therefore ten percent of your readers – have some form of dyslexia or reading difficulty, so you want to make the layout as user-friendly as possible.

Paragraphs should be split as follows:

- In dialogue: when a new character speaks.

And a new section (blank line then first non-indented paragraph, subsequent paragraphs should then be indented two or three spaces)…

- when another character becomes the main point of view character;
- when time has passed and it's not necessary to tell us what happened in between because it's not relevant to the plot.

NOTES:

112. Past vs passed

Generally 'past' refers to time whereas 'passed' is usually a verb, the past tense of 'to pass' which refers to movement, although you can say 'Tom moved past the door' which is movement but 'past' in this case is not the verb, 'to move' is. To help you, think of past tense being a historical time.

113. PC or not PC

Is there something in your writing that isn't 'politically correct'? I've been shot down (I would say 'in flames' but it's a cliché) on social media (Facebook mostly) for voicing an opinion that some didn't disagree with. I'm no rebel but there will always be someone who disagrees with something you say.

Unless you are writing with a particular audience in mind, don't write to offend or disgust. I've judged (oh yes, I'm a competition judge too including the BBC Radio 2 500-word stories) stories where they haven't stuck to a given theme and had particular violence (or characters being sick for no reason!). I'm no prude – I'm a crime and romance writer – but those stories leapt out… for all the wrong reasons.

114. Poetry – alliteration and rhythm

Alliteration – that's 'Peter Piper picked a peck of pickled pepper' – is a key feature of poems, and while you wouldn't use it to that extent in your prose, how words sound is very important. As I've said elsewhere in this book, I recommend you read out your writing as it helps you spot mistakes. Not only that but it is a way of you testing how the rhythm sounds. I'm sure you've heard stories (or poems) before where it sounds like the soothing rhythm of a train… if you find trains soothing.

115. Points of view

I did cover this topic early in this book but worth having its own entry here because it's such an important feature to get right.

In each story, or section of a novel's chapter, there should just be one main point of view, especially when writing in first person.

If you need to switch from another character's viewpoint,

then leave a blank line and start a new section where the first paragraph will be flush to the left then subsequent paragraphs indented two or three spaces. You would do this too when there is a gap in time.

Possessive items – see 'Apostrophes'

116. Pronouns – also see 'Sentence construction'

A pronoun is 'he', 'she', 'the', and the character's name. I talk about not having too many later (in Sentence construction) so this is about not having too many hes, shes or names.

Purple prose – see 'Word choice'

117. Questions

How often do you ask questions in your writing? By having a character ask a question or query something in thoughts (also see 'Characters – thinking'), it makes your reader think and question themselves. What you don't want is for the reader to come out of the story enough for them to stop but making them think can only (hopefully!) be a good thing.

NOTES:

118. Read aloud

Have you read your writing out loud? This is where critique writing groups excel at because not only can others feed back on your 'mistakes' but you can often spot them this way too.

You might not want to read your whole novel to yourself out loud but if a passage isn't working or you're struggling with it for whatever reason, then reading aloud will help.

Alternatively for those of you with a Kindle with text-to-speech (a Mac will do the same), I find it really useful having someone else (even an automated voice) reading my work back to me.

You are more likely to hear the mistakes that your eyes don't pick up.

119. Read other people's books

Some writers won't read books of a similar genre when they are writing their own in case they plagiarise by accident. I have a terrible memory so unless I wrote it down, I wouldn't include something I read.

https://www.grammarly.com/plagiarism is a free checker and https://en.wikipedia.org/wiki/Plagiarism explains the topic further.

By reading other books, regardless of our genres or not, it helps you with the elements of your own writing because of the sentence construction, pacing, description and dialogue.

They will help you to see ultimately what works and more importantly what doesn't work. Why do you enjoy or dislike a story?

120. Repetition

Repetition should only be used for emphasis, e.g. 'Andy got in the car. There was no sign of his wife. He honked the horn of the car.' Although you've mentioned another noun (wife) after the first 'car', we know that it won't refer to his wife. Removing the 'of the car' will still let what is said make perfect sense.

An example of repetition that works is, 'He stood under the old oak tree, a tree so huge that its shadow eclipsed the building opposite.'

121. Research

It (almost) goes without saying that you must do your research. Get something wrong and there will be a reader out there who knows more about your topic than you do. At best, it will frustrate them. At worst, they will stop reading, switch to their email system and let you know that you've got something wrong.

Only put as much as the story needs. Don't be tempted to include everything as it will come across as showing off and the reader will lose interest if it distracts them from the amazing plot you've created.

122. Round vs around

Generally, if a character turns 'around' they do so in a full circle, i.e. 360 degrees. If they turn to face someone, they turn round rather than around.

123. Said or asked

When the end of a piece of dialogue has a question mark, the dialogue tag (if one is needed) is usually 'asked', e.g. "Does my bum look big in this?" she asked. (Always a bad question to ask!)

If what is said is more of a statement, e.g. "It's cold today, isn't it." then said is fine. Better still, have description, e.g. Tom twirled. "Does my bum look big in this?"

NOTES:

124. Said she vs she said

http://words.journalism.ku.edu/attribute.html favours the usual 'she said' although it adds, "Place the attribution before the speaker's name only when the name is followed by a long identification, an appositive or a non-restrictive clause, e.g. The train had sounded its whistle and had flares burning on the back car, **said** H.D. Muldoon, a brakeman on the train who witnessed the crash, or The train had sounded its whistle and had flares burning on the back car, H.D. Muldoon, a brakeman on the train, **said.**".

I much prefer 'she said' as it is much more natural but it's up to you and while 'said she' is more of a historical choice, you may feel it suits your story better.

125. Scriptwriting

Even if you're not considering writing a script, I would recommend trying the format because it is great practice for dialogue. The self-proclaimed 'web's largest movie script resource' http://www.imsdb.com has almost every script available including the 2017 hit http://www.imsdb.com/scripts/La-La-Land.html.

An example of a script extract (not a real one) is:

JANE

What did he do when you told him?

SOPHIA

What do you think?

Jane leans forward, towards Sophia, and takes Sophia's right hand.

JANE

Freaked.

Sophia laughs and holds out her left hand.

SOPHIA

He asked me to marry him!

Both girls scream.

***

There is less narration (description) and the plot concentrates on what is said between the characters.

Take a scene from your current (or previously finished) project and read out the dialogue only, i.e. with no 'he said', 'she said', description etc. and see whether it works.

Could you rewrite your novel as a script?

126. Seats – into or onto

It's often said (written) that a character will get into a seat (e.g. he got into the back seat of the car) but that could make your reader think that they're lifting up the seat and climbing in. Instead, you would want to say, 'He got onto the back seat of the car'. That doesn't sound quite right though, does it. Do you have to be that specific? Just have them get into the back of the car. Because they're entering the car then 'into' is fine.

NOTES:

127. Sentence construction – beginnings

Think about how your sentences are constructed. Most stories start with too many pronouns, e.g. He / she / the characters names. Try turning the sentence round, e.g. 'Stepping off the ledge, Sandy…' Or more simply, 'As Sandy stepped off the ledge. You don't want to do that too many times though. Have a mixture of starts. Pick a page and read out the first word of each sentence. If more than four are the same then look at changing some of them.

128. Sentence construction – endings

Generally, the impact should be at the end of the sentences so it leaves a ghost of emotion before the reader continues. If a section isn't working look at the construction of the sentences and see where you feel the impact lies. Can you change the order of the sentence so the most powerful word is the final one?

129. Sentence lengths

Short sentences make for snappy prose, that is that the pace of the story will quicken the shorter the sentences, and more impact on your readers, e.g. Not at all.

130. Set up vs set-up

'set up' is a verb, e.g. 'She set up the tables' whereas a 'set-up' is a noun, e.g. 'He knew that the set-up has been elaborate'.

131. Shouted ~~out~~

When a character shouts, they're not generally shouting internally, to themselves, but aloud so you don't need the 'out'.

132. Showing not telling

You may have heard of the phrase 'show not tell' or 'show don't tell'. If I only gave you one tip it would be this one. A 'tell' is the narrator telling us what happened. A 'show' is having the character doing the action or speaking.

An example of this would be:

> Tell: Andy was angry.
> Show: “Get out!” Andy slammed the door.

133. Side to side or side-to-side

http://www.thefreedictionary.com/side-to-side lists the latter and I'm inclined to agree although other resources drop the hyphens.

134. Sir

Unless someone really is a sir, e.g. Sir Ben Kingsley, then one character being polite to another would call them ‘sir’ (with a small s).

Slang – see ‘Accents, slang etc.’

135. Sometime vs some time

While they both relate to a non-specific amount of time, the easiest way to remember the difference is if you can replace ‘some’ with ‘a’, then you’re using the right one. If you said, ‘They promised to meet up sometime’ then ‘They promised to meet up a time’ wouldn’t make sense, whereas if you said ‘Some time earlier, they’d promised to meet’, you could say ‘A time earlier, they’d promised to meet’.

NOTES:

136. Span vs spun

'Span' means the distance between two points and is often used as the past tense of 'to spin' but that should be 'spun', although 'span' used to be used for the latter and as http://english.stackexchange.com/questions/23404/which-is-the-correct-past-tense-of-spin-span-or-spun says, it has fallen out of favour to be replaced by spun.

Speech marks vs inverted commas – see 'inverted commas'.

137. Spell and grammar check

This may seem obvious but have you spell and grammar checked your novel? It's easy to do it when you've first finished but do remember to do it again before you submit it anywhere. That said, a spell-checker (the red squiggly lines in Word) and grammar check (green lines) will only go so far. Reading aloud (as mentioned above) will help with the grammar. Most common mistakes include there (a place), their (belonging to them) and they're (they are) – easily done but something that points you out to a judge or editor, again for the wrong reason.

138. Split infinitives

Wherever possible try not to split your infinitives. In other words where you have a verb like 'to dig out' try and have 'He dug out the address book' rather than 'He dug the address book out'. It's only a little thing but it usually sounds cleaner. Of course there are instances where it's not possible to do that, e.g. 'He threw the glove down on to the table.' The verb is to throw down but you wouldn't say 'He threw down the glove on to the table'. You could but it doesn't sound quite right.

139. Stared vs starred

If a character is looking at someone or something intently then it's 'stared' but if he or she appeared in a play, then they 'starred' in it.

Started to – see Began to / started to

140. Stationary vs stationery

Stationary is the verb (e.g. the car is stationary) whereas stationery is paper, pens etc.

141. Still

'still' is another word that is often repeated unnecessarily. If you search for it, check that you don't have any too close together. The chances are that you will keep the ones that mean unmoving but not so often with the ones that mean yet (time or quantity).

142. Stories vs storeys

Tales are stories (story singular), levels in a building are storeys (storey singular). An easy mistake to make.

143. Swearing

I'm often asked whether it is okay to have swearing in your writing. It is, providing it is in keeping with the context within the story. An example I give is that if a burglar was shinning up a drainpipe and it came away from the wall. He wouldn't say "bother" as he fell but would swear. Depending upon your audience you'd either put in the swearing (if you're writing a dark crime where the reader would expect a dark side), but if you're writing for a Christian, clean, or young audience then you would just have 'he swore'. You want to choose the route that doesn't make the reader stop reading.

NOTES:

144. Synopsise your novel

Regardless of whether you are going to self-publish or to submit to an agent or publisher, you'll need a synopsis. It's very helpful to have a synopsis before you write as it will help you plan your story, even if you don't know everything that happens from A-Z. You can fill the missing sections in as the story develops. Writing (or amending) a synopsis at the end of your first draft will help you ensure that the story works!

I would recommend, however, that you write a short paragraph as you finish each chapter, e.g. Chapter 12: Gordon reaches the church but learns that Robert left the day before. He has to go back to the library for more research. (That's not one of my plots, by the way, or any other that I know of, so feel free to use it!).

Write it in present tense as your synopsis for submission (or upload to Amazon etc. if self-publishing) will be in present tense.

145. Take out the detail

Although every scene needs some detail, you don't have to have someone taking every step from the bathroom or kitchen to the bedroom. This is where you can leave a paragraph space and start the next scene, like you would in a script (although the format of that is more complex, I wrote one for now-defunct Script Frenzy in 2010).

And don't 'pad'. If your book is too short don't add in content that you've already said elsewhere (and certainly if you're tempted to add a 'tell' when you've already 'shown' us what's happening).

These days with eBooks, the length of the book doesn't matter as long as it's good and you've not left anything important out (e.g. tying up all the loose ends by the final page). The best way to add content is by adding another character and / or dilemma.

Rita Kuehn gives some great advice on adding http://writania.com/one-collective-final-mush-to-finish-well-in-nanowrimo-2012.

146. Their, there, and they're

One of the most commonly confused word spellings are these three. Their is a possessive word, e.g. their jackets are dirty. There refers to a place or quantity, e.g. there are three jackets. They're is a shortening of they are, e.g. They're going to collect their dirty jackets.

147. This vs that

Like today, tonight, and tomorrow, when you're writing in present tense then 'this' is fine, but when writing in past tense you would say 'that', e.g. 'Tyler thought that was a stupid idea' rather than 'Tyler thought this was a stupid idea.' Dialogue, however, is different. You would use present tense in dialogue, unless a character is reminiscing.

148. Three is a magic number

Sets of three work really well. Phrases have a rhythm to them when they include a set of three, e.g. 'Sam slumped on to the chair, picked up his mug, and shouted at the television.' It may not feel like a set but think about what you already have that is a threesome!

149. Timing – tenses

If you are writing in present tense, then going back in time would usually be simple past tense, e.g. 'he walks' to 'he walked'. If you're writing in past tense, the going back would be to 'past perfect', e.g. 'he walked' to 'he had walked'. https://learnenglish.britishcouncil.org/en/english-grammar/verbs in this case – is a fabulous resource on this topic.

NOTES:

150. Timing – products

Be careful of using product model numbers because it will date your writing. If you are setting your story in a particular period of history then that's fine but, like a plastic water bottle appearing on the mantelpiece in a scene of Downton Abbey (http://www.thenimbusproject.com/?p=1661 tells us that they didn't exist commercially before 1947 and Downton Abbey is set between 1912 and 1925), you have to ensure that the items were available at the time. You can be vague. For example, have the characters using an iPhone rather than iPhone 4, driving a BMW M series rather than BMW M3.

151. Titles

By the time you have finished your first draft, you probably already have your title – maybe you had your title before doing any writing – but does it fit? Like a title on any project, and as the saying goes, it does what it says on the tin; it has to represent the story.

I wrote a short story a day from May 2015 for over a year so had to come up with a lot of titles. Quite often there would be a word or phrase in the story that I felt perfect.

If you self-publish then it's important to pick a great title. It still is if submitting to a magazine or website (for a short story) or agent or publisher (novel or story / poetry collections) but the chances are that one or both of them will want to change the title/s so don't be too precious about it.

The same goes for a book's cover. If you are looking to design your own (I also design book covers – see https://morgenbailey.wordpress.com/cover-design).

You shouldn't have, for example, a dog on the front cover if there's no mention of a dog inside it!

Again, a publisher will likely choose their own cover so you don't need to create your own unless self-publishing.

Titles aren't copyright so you can use someone else's but try and make it more interesting than something like 'The Journey'. I changed a story I'd written called that to 'No White Left'… much better.

152. Today, tonight, tomorrow

When writing in present tense, it's fine to say something happens today, tonight or tomorrow but in past tense they're no longer today (that day), tonight (that evening), or tomorrow (the following day / the next day / a day later). Likewise, yesterday should be the day before / the previous day / a day earlier, last week = the previous week etc.

Dialogue, however, is different. You would use present tense in dialogue, unless a character is reminiscing.

153. to that

'to that' at the end, for example, of someone saying nothing removes the impact of the 'nothing', especially where it ends a sentence. Generally, the impact should be at the end of the sentences so it leaves a ghost of emotion before the reader continues.

154. Tough, through, though, thought

These four words look very similar on the page. I've mentioned a few times throughout this book about the importance of reading your writing aloud, or better still getting someone (or something; a Kindle or computer's text-to-speech function) to do so, ideally when you are there with them, and it's never more true when you have words that look this alike.

NOTES:

155. Toward vs towards

http://www.quickanddirtytips.com/education/grammar/toward-versus-towards?page=all explains that, on the whole, us Brits say 'towards' and Americans say "toward".

156. Twenty-four seven or 24/7

As I mentioned earlier, I'm always in favour of using text rather than digits and while you can use the latter, I'd recommend going with twenty-four seven (or alternatives like 'continuous').

157. UK vs US

I have mentioned this before but worth looking at in more detail. To colour or color? when is a bonnet a hood? In theory it depends on who you are aiming your piece at. If it's going to be published in a US magazine then you'd generally go with US (ditto UK for UK) but if you're character is American they're going to call a bonnet a hood.

My chick lit novel is set in Northampton, England and Izzy is from the UK so everything is British English.

As long as the reader can understand and everything is realistic (accents, phrases etc) then go with whatever works (but do check your facts if you're outside your postal or comfort zone!).

NB. Keep your accents to a minimum. If a reader can't understand what your character it saying, you'll lose them.

Up to date vs up-to-date – see 'Hand in hand'

158. Verbs (also see 'Adverbs' and 'Continual verbs')

Verbs are usually action, a character doing something. Try and make them as interesting as you can. Why have a character walking when you could have them ambling, plodding, shuffling, or sprinting? Your readers will have good imaginations but the more vivid you make your descriptions, and dialogue realistic, the better.

159. Versions and backup

I'd recommend every time you make major changes to a document, you save it as a later version e.g. 'Tall Ships v1.0' then …1.1 etc. (obviously saving the original first), so you always have earlier versions should you remove something in a later version and need to get it back.

You can also keep your writing securely online (e.g. Cloud Drive, Dropbox etc) in case anything happens to your computer. And backup regularly, every day at least.

160. Voice

You may have heard of the phrase 'authorial voice'. This is one way a reader can distinguish your writing from anyone else's. It's easier to have an authorial voice in first person narration because the character is going to have an attitude. Doing so in third person is more difficult because the equivalent is for the narrator to have an opinion or remark on the character's opinion. My favourite film 'Stranger than Fiction' (which most people have never heard of but features Will Ferrell, Emma Thompson, Dustin Hoffman, Queen Latifah, and Maggie Gyllenhaal) has loads of authorial voice (quite literally). I won't plot spoil but there's an ongoing battle between the character and narrator. It's so clever. An example in this film is when Will and Dustin chat about 'Little Did He Know' where there is something the reader learns but the character him/herself doesn't know yet. It can only be a second or two difference but reader love to be kept in the loop… as the cliché goes!

NOTES:

161. Wander vs wonder

'wander' means to walk without purpose whereas 'wonder' to be curious about something. You can have your character wonder about wandering around with a wand. ☺

162. Was vs were (subjunctive)

If I was or if I were? The latter is correct and http://www.quickanddirtytips.com/education/grammar/subjunctive-verbs explains this.

163. Way too many ways

Another I've noticed is how many words end in 'way'. There have been sentences (or paragraphs) with way, away, and doorway in them. This is not necessarily noticeable on the page but have the work read out and it will become more evident. Choose, then, your words wisely.

While vs whilst – see Among vs amongst

164. Who vs whom

There are loads of sites out there discussing when to use 'who' and when to use 'whom'. These include: http://www.quickanddirtytips.com/education/grammar/who-versus-whom?page=all which says, 'who' when the main person, the subject, is being talked about or doing the action and 'whom' when the secondary person, the object, is being talked about). There is also http://www.grammarbook.com/grammar/whovwhom.asp, http://www.elearnenglishlanguage.com/difficulties/whowhom.html and http://www.prdaily.com/Main/Articles/Who_vs_whom_A_simple_trick_for_determining_when_to_8964.aspx, the latter of which says, "Figure it out by... replacing the who or whom with he or him. If he is wrong, so is who. If him is wrong, so is whom.

165. Who's vs whose

The easy way of remembering which is which here is that the shortening of who's means 'who is'. If swapping the who's for who is doesn't make sense then it's going to be 'whose'. 'Who's' usually precedes a verb, e.g. 'Who's going?' whereas 'whose' usually precedes a noun, e.g. 'Whose shoes are they?'

166. Word choice

This guide is mainly for short story authors and novelists but the words you choose still matter. Poets love alliteration, e.g. Peter Piper picked a peck of pickled pepper…, although you don't want to be as comedic unless writing a comedy.

Although your reader will be concentrating on the story rather than how it's written, you still want it to be the best that it can be. Like adverbs and descriptive verbs, why have plain when you can have stunning words. Don't go mad and make it 'purple prose' which, as explains, 'In literary criticism, purple prose is prose text that is so extravagant, ornate, or flowery as to break the flow and draw excessive attention to itself. Purple prose is characterized by the extensive use of adjectives, adverbs, and metaphors. When it is limited to certain passages, they may be termed purple patches or purple passages, standing out from the rest of the work.' See https://en.wikipedia.org/wiki/Purple_prose for the entire article.

NOTES:

167. Word count

How long is your story? Wikipedia has a list of word counts at https://en.wikipedia.org/wiki/Word_count as follows:

Classification	Word count
Novel	over 40,000 words*
Novella	17,500 to 40,000 words
Novelette	7,500 to 17,500 words
Short story	under 7,500 words

There is also flash fiction (usually 300-1000) and micro-fiction (up to 300 words). * This matrix will help you classify your story when submitting it, although I don't agree with the novel word count as most publishers will consider this to still be a novella.

The average size novel is 80,000 to 90,000 words but don't worry if your first draft is longer than that. Ideally it should be, as you'd likely chop up to ten percent during the editing process. What you don't want to be is a lot shorter than that and be tempted to pad it out just to take it to what you think it should be.

Word counts will vary depending upon your genre. If you are writing a science fiction / fantasy novel then is likely to be longer. What you don't want to do is produce a novella and sent it to agents or publishers who only represent / publish novels of the standard word count and above.

A bit of useful information for you… if you are self-publishing your book with CreateSpace:

- anything up to 108 pages in the larger 6"x9" size or the smaller 5"x8" format (the same size as this book) should cost the same.
- any book smaller than 133 pages is too thin to have the title / author on the spine. That's why I made sure this was that length (totalling 24,816 words).

I'd recommend the 5"x8" anyway as it fits more bookshelves, and some bookshop shelves are designed for that size.

168. Words that mean the same

I've sometimes come across words that mean the same which means one could come out, e.g. but nevertheless… While they're not exactly the same, we don't need both. Use whichever you feel is best in the context.

169. Wordy phrases

Why use three words (or more) when one will do… take a look at http://www.dailywritingtips.com/50-plain-language-substitutions-for-wordy-phrases for 50 examples.

170. Why use five words when one will do

Think about the words and phrases you use. You want your writing to be concise so as this item says, why use four words when one will do. For example, choose 'they look alike' instead of 'they look that close to each other.'

171. Zzz…

Don't forget to do a final spell and grammar check.

NOTES:

The layout of your book

Paragraphs and indents

I have some layout topics already but here are some more specifics…

The layout should be the same as a traditionally published book. Take any book from your burgeoning* shelf and see how it has been laid out. *As a writer you should also be a reader. The first paragraph of the section should be flush to the left then subsequent paragraphs indented by two or three spaces. An example is below:

> **Full Moon**
>
> Swinging the gate open, Jody winced as it complained. Looking up at her parents' bedroom she waited for a light.
>
> Above the house, the moon was bright and whole, splintered by next door's Leylandii. She smiled as she thought of the scene from Bruce Almighty where Jim Carrey enlarges the moon and pulls it closer.
>
> With the house still in darkness, she put her key in the lock, slowly, silently, and held the handle as she pushed the door away from its frame, closing it again just as quietly. Climbing the stairs she avoided the step that creaked.
>
> In the bubble of her room, she leant against the windowsill staring out into the night. She could hear her father snoring next door and she smiled as she imagined her mother's efforts getting to sleep.
>
> Jody was making shapes out of the stars when she felt a finger jab her back.

You will see that there's a break between the third and fourth paragraphs. This is because time has passed and rather than say, in this instance, that Jody went to the bathroom, brushed her teeth, got ready for bed etc. we just have her in her bedroom with how she got there assumed by the reader. Whatever isn't vital to the story can be left out.

Fonts

The standard font is Times New Roman font size 12 but it's not very viewer friendly because it is a serif font. (It's got appendages on its letters.)

This book has been written in… <coughs> that's indirect action! <slaps wrist> I have written this book in Arial which you will see is quite a soft font with no curly letters or sharp edges.

Line spacing

The standard spacing for a manuscript is double-spaced. A synopsis and cover letter would usually be single-spaced. You could go somewhere in between; this book is single spaced but has '2 pt' spacing 'After' (Format / Paragraph on the top toolbar).

Chapter endings

I recommend having a symbol indicating the end of each chapter. The 'norm' on manuscripts is three asterisks, e.g.

***

…but publishers will change them to whatever they prefer. You could also put one asterisk (instead of just a blank line) between sections during the chapter where you change point of view, there is a gap in time, or go back in time.

And finally… an overview

So, when writing a story (of any length) think about...

- Is the main character likeable? Even if he or she isn't, the reader has to care what happens to them.
- Unless it's flash fiction, do you have a start, middle and end?
- Does the ending work? If you're writing a sequel, you can leave sub-plots left open to be resolved subsequently but the main plot will usually be tied up, or at least hinted at. Or vice versa; the sub-plots are resolved but the main plot will be resolved thereafter.
- Is there enough action for the reader to be wanting to read on?
- Are you showing more than you're telling? You should have as much as possible from the character's perspective, i.e. 'Jackie screwed up her nose at the prospect of doing it again.' Rather than have the narrator tell us that she didn't like the prospect of doing it again.
- Have you checked that you don't have too many sentences starting with a pronoun (he / she / name)?
- Do you have any negatives? We write about what's there but what about something that's missing, e.g. an empty supermarket car park in the middle of the day.

- Have you avoided repetition unless it's to emphasise the first instance? Sets of three work well.

- Have you checked your points of view and tenses?

- Do you have a mix of sentence lengths? Long sentences slow the pace, short ones quicken it.

- Do you have the five senses? You won't always have taste, touch and smell (as well as sight and sound) but if you can get them in (naturally), all the better.

- Do you have plenty of colour? Try to use russet, scarlet etc rather than red.

- Is everything relevant? Do you have a scene where nothing really happens? Everything has to progress the plot or reveal character.

- Read your work aloud. Does anything jar with you? Get someone else to read your story, to themselves or aloud. For those of you with Kindle Fires, email your story to it (it'll be something like john_1234@kindle.com) then use the text-to-speech function to have the story read back to you. Mistakes become all the more glaring that way.

And finally… specifics

You've finished your first draft and you want to do a quick sweep before you sit down and go line by line through your manuscript. Now do these tweaks…

- Language set to your country (Tools / Language)
- adverbs: tightly, slowly, quickly etc. (replace with more active / interesting verbs)
- chop clichés
- thoughts in italics
- The – (hyphen) separating phrases changed to – (dash)
- excess words: usually, normally, especially, that, every, just, complete / completely, total / totally, entire / entirely, absolute / absolutely, really, very, right, simply, immediately etc.
- nodded ~~his / her head~~, shrugged ~~his / her shoulders~~
- chop the 'at all's that aren't used for emphasis
- unnecessary 'he said's when you have description
- each character speaking has their own paragraph
- numbers under 100 as text (unless titles etc.)
- ago vs before / earlier
- ok changed to okay
- it's vs its
- maybe vs may be
- Mum vs my mum
- they're, their, or there
- you include as many of the five senses as possible
- too many clichés
- too much narration vs character doing / saying
- the ending ties everything (unless writing a series)
- he / she refers to the last noun mentioned
- one main character point of view per section
- mix of sentence lengths (short add pace)
- showing not telling

I'd be delighted to hear from you if this book has helped you and you'd like me to edit your novel – or just provide feedback, or something in between –
see my blog's Editing and Critique page (https://morgenbailey.wordpress.com/editing-and-critique).

Is your editor worth it? Or not?
There's a very interesting article on editors on http://publishingperspectives.com/2015/01/editor-worth-not.

I'm not sure I agree with the 'love/hate relationship' but editing is a tough task to do to your own writing (not so for me with my clients' books; I love pulling them apart) but hopefully this guide has helped you.

As I said earlier, everyone needs an editor so while this guide has been designed to help you buff your masterpiece, it won't replace a second (third, or fourth, or more!) opinion.

When everything's done
When you're happy with your book… or as happy as you can be… then it can go. I have lists of various outlets for various formats (novels, stories, poems, scripts, non-fiction etc.) within the Submission information area of my blog (https://morgenbailey.wordpress.com/submission-information). Good luck!

Free eBook offer
Before you find out more about me, as a 'thank you' for purchasing the paperback version of this guide, I would like to send you the latest electronic (mobi, pdf, or epub) version. I am regularly updating this guide so the electronic version may well have more content.

To take up this offer, send me proof of purchase (or where you bought it if directly from me) and a photograph of you reading the guide so I can add it to my blog. Thank you!

About the Author

Morgen Bailey is a writing-related blogger who spotlights authors, agents, editors and publishers. Other content includes guest posts, flash fiction, poetry, and short story and writing guide reviews.

She is also a freelance editor and offers a free 1,000-word sample edit to all new enquirers.

She runs a free monthly 100-word competition and has been a judge for various competitions including the annual H.E. Bates Short Story Competition (2015), NLG Flash Fiction Competition (2013-4), RONE (2015), and BBC Radio 2 500-word Competition (2016-7).

The author of numerous short stories, novels, articles, she has also dabbled with poetry.

Morgen teaches creative writing across Northamptonshire (and beyond), belongs to three local writing groups, is a charity shop volunteer, a regular cinema visitor, reads (though not as often as she'd like), and in between she writes.

Everything she's involved in is detailed on her blog http://morgenbailey.wordpress.com. She can also be found chatting away about all things literary on Twitter, Facebook, LinkedIn and Tumblr.

To contact her you can also complete
her website's 'Contact me' page
or email her at morgen@morgenbailey.com.

Discover other titles by Morgen Bailey at
https://morgenbailey.wordpress.com/books-mine.

Photographs courtesy of pixabay.com.
Cover design, internal layout etc.
by Morgen Bailey.

Note from the Author

Thank you for purchasing
'The Writer's Guide to Editing Fiction'.

I'd like to take this opportunity to also thank my writing friends – especially Joy (and other Northants Authors members), Tony, Jane, and Pat, and everyone involved in Crime & Publishment, Gretna Green, Scotland – for their ongoing support.

I welcome feedback (and am always grateful for honest reviews) and you can either find me on social media as morgenwriteruk and / or via email: morgen@morgenbailey.com.

Throughout this book I gave you spaces to make notes but just in case you wanted more space to write new ideas or even just for your shopping list or all those jobs you have to do before you sit down and write...

NOTES:

Just like a secret final track on an album…

Thank you again for buying this book, I hope you feel it has been worth every penny, cent, yen, franc, dollar, peso, colon, kuna, krone, nakfa, birr, gourde, dinar…

Have fun with your writing and again, let me know how you get on.

morgen@morgenbailey.com

71145742R00083

Made in the USA
Columbia, SC
25 May 2017